An Illustrated History of
EDINBURGH'S RAILWAYS

Classic view of Waverley in the 1960s.

by
W.A.C. Smith & Paul Anderson

IRWELL
PRESS

ACKNOWLEDGEMENTS

The authors would like to thank F.W. Shuttleworth for processing the photographs. All are the copyright of W.A.C. Smith unless otherwise credited. They also wish to thank Barry Osborn of Leicester for typesetting the maps, Mick George of Loughborough for producing bromides and Allison Bennett of Coalville for photocopying work. Also, thanks to W.S. Sellar for providing photographs of the St. Leonards branch and Gullane. W.A.C. Smith would also like to pay especial thanks to Doris for her interest, encouragement and patience, to say nothing of considerable practical help, during the preparation of this book.

First published in the U.K. by Irwell Press,
P.O. Box 1260, Caernarfon, Gwynedd, LL55 3ZD
Printed by The Amadeus Press, Huddersfield

Contents

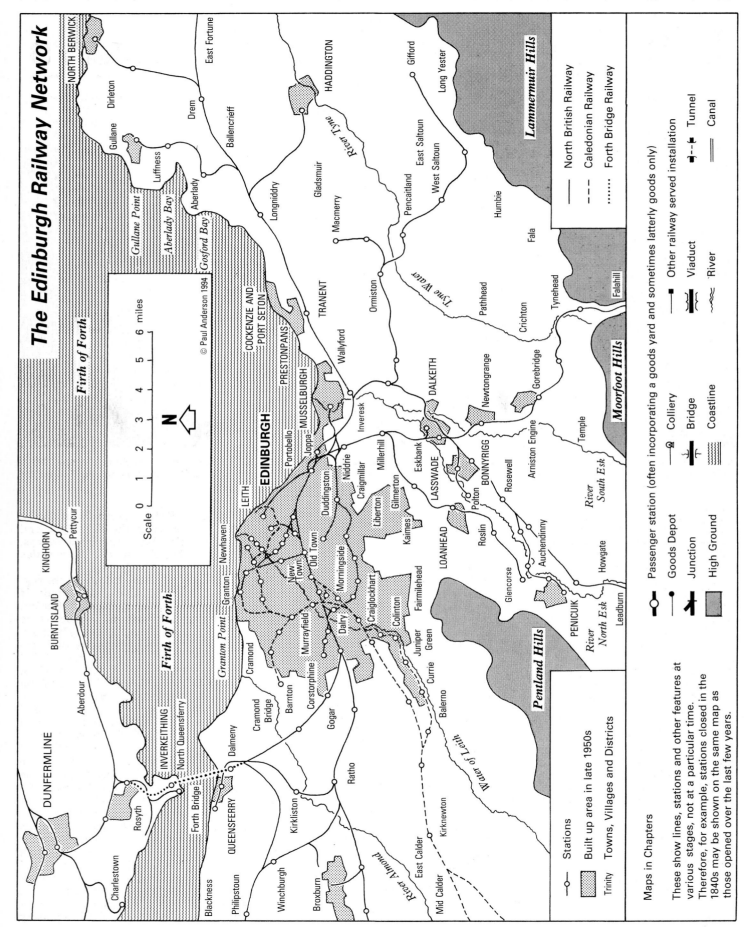

The Edinburgh Railway Network

© Paul Anderson 1994

Scale

0 1 2 3 4 5 6 miles

N

Firth of Forth

Lammermuir Hills

Moorfoot Hills

Pentland Hills

North British Railway

Caledonian Railway

Forth Bridge Railway

Other railway served installation

Viaduct

Tunnel

River

Canal

Passenger station (often incorporating a goods yard and sometimes latterly goods only)

Goods Depot

Junction

Colliery

Bridge

Coastline

High Ground

Stations

Built up area in late 1950s

Trinity   Towns, Villages and Districts

Maps in Chapters

These show lines, stations and other features at various stages, not at a particular time. Therefore, for example, stations closed in the 1840s may be shown on the same map as those opened over the last few years.

4

Introduction

Edinburgh and its Railways

If there is one scene which characterises Edinburgh's railways, it is the view of Waverley station from above The Mound tunnel. With Princes Street Gardens to the left and North Bridge in the background, V2 2-6-2 No.60804 pulled out of the capital with the 5.05pm for Aberdeen on 5th July 1958.

Edinburgh itself hardly needs an introduction, for once seen it is never forgotten. It has by far the most spectacular centre of any city in the British Isles and scores highly even on a world scale. Castle Rock, the Old Town, Princes Street, the Gardens, Calton Hill, the New Town and Arthur's Seat combine to create a fascinating urban landscape, and even the railways made a contribution, with two impressive hotels. The capital of Scotland has been involved with virtually every phase of the country's history. It has experienced violence and sieges on the one hand, but has been home to some of the greatest philosophers and scientists on the other. Thousands of tenement chimneys in the Old Town prompted the not unaffectionate nickname 'Auld Reekie' whilst the unfinished National Monument on Calton Hill helped give rise the sobriquet 'Athens of the North'. Even Edinburgh's hinterland has a wealth of interest and variety. To the north is the mighty Firth of Forth with its bridges, former ferry crossings, little fishing harbours, popular holiday resorts, and great port of Leith. To the south lie the Pentland and Moorfoot Hills, rich farmland, some exquisite mill villages, the wooded clefts carved by Water of Leith and the North

Esk and what was once one of Scotland's most productive coalfields. The city itself is particularly lively and vibrant nowadays, and the annual Edinburgh International Festival of Music and Drama helps make it one of Europe's premier tourist destinations.

Geological diversity combined with the effects of the Ice Age have been paramount in shaping the scenery in and around Edinburgh. A great body of limestone, sandstone and shale stretching from Queensferry to Aberlady makes up most of the plateau surrounding the city, but around Dalkeith and Bonnyrigg it is comprised of coal seams. At the Southern Boundary Fault, running south westwards from Dunbar, these rocks give way to hard slates forming the Lammermuir and Moorfoot Hills, as well as the uplands around Peebles. Volcanic activity added further details to the landscape. Extensive lava flows make up the Pentland Hills and the rough ground around North Berwick, whilst the cores of ancient volcanoes form prominent outcrops such as Castle Rock, Arthur's Seat, North Berwick Law and the Ferry Hills at North Queensferry. Glaciers pushing eastwards deposited debris forming the slope occupied by the Old Town and also gouged out a great hollow, later flooded by sea water

to create the Firth of Forth. Since the Ice Age, rivers such as the Esk, Tyne and Water of Leith have carved out valleys, adding further elements to the complex surface of the Lothians.

Edinburgh owes its existence to the rugged crag on which the Castle stands. It commanded the sea approach to Central Scotland from the east and overlooked the main route north marched by the Romans, Saxons and English. A Pictish castle existed in the 5th century and about 1,300 years ago this elevated site became known as Dun Edin, Gaelic for 'fortress of the hill slope', thus giving the city its name. The castle was a favourite residence of Scottish kings from the 11th century and following the defeat of Macbeth became the capital in 1124, when the village of Edinburgh was established outside the walls. Another little settlement, called Canongate, grew up close to the new Holy Rood Abbey below Arthur's Seat. After the fierce War of Independence in 1329, victorious Robert the Bruce merged the two burghs and gave the city control over the port of Leith. For a century and a half Edinburgh was beset by feuds, battles and assassinations, but talented James IV coming to the throne in 1488 heralded a golden but short lived era. Over the next twenty years he introduced a Compulsory

Edinburgh and its hinterland is enormously varied and the railway system reflected this. Apart from five main routes served by two fine city centre stations, it had a fairly comprehensive suburban system, some delightful rural branches, lines to the seaside, a complex dock network and of course the Forth Bridge. There was also the pioneering Edinburgh & Dalkeith Railway, originally horse operated. Although most of it was substantially rebuilt after being absorbed by the North British Railway, the section from Duddingston to St. Leonards retained its character, notably the hefty stone boundary walls. In bright sunshine, J35 0-6-0 No.64486 hammered past the flanks of Arthur's Seat with the branch goods on 19th October 1955, in a second attempt to climb the gradient. Photograph W.S. Sellar.

Education Act, established the Royal College of Surgeons and gave Scotland its first printing press. Edinburgh had become a city of European stature, but the English resumed raids across the border. The conflict culminated in the Battle of Flodden at the base of the Cheviots during 1513 when James died along with 10,000 of his men in the worst ever Scottish defeat. Edinburgh was terrified of attack; a new wall around the city was begun but the invasion never came.

Instead, the fighting was internal, with great families squabbling for supremacy and one outcome was a bloody battle in the Royal Mile, between the Castle and Holyrood, during 1520. Meanwhile the infant King James V was imprisoned in the Castle before escaping to Stirling. Just before his death in 1542 he became the father of Mary Queen of Scots and her colourful and tragic life has captured the imagination of the world ever since. Henry VIII failed to marry her to his son and embarked on the violent raids on central Scotland known as the 'Rough Wooing'. She spent twelve years exiled in France and prompted the 'monstrous regimen of women' comment by reformer John Knox after her return. Her flight to seek asylum in England after the Battle of Langside near Glasgow led to imprisonment and eventual execution by her cousin Queen Elizabeth during 1587. Her son became James I of England in 1603 and with the Union of the Crowns, Edinburgh effectively ceased to be a royal capital.

At the time, the city was still a crowded, medieval settlement, tumbling down from the Castle. Wynds, closes and entries led off the Royal Mile amongst huge buildings consisting of house piled upon house, in effect forming vertical streets. Away from the city, farming and fishing were paramount, although water-powered grain, flax, paper and snuff mills were active alongside the Water of Leith and River Esk. Coal pits supplied fuel and it was these that prompted the early railways. As early as 1606 a wooden waggonway was planned at Inveresk to carry coal down to the sea, although there is no firm evidence that it was actually built. The late 1600s were an unsettled time for Edinburgh with protest and rioting over the proposed Union, culminating in a siege of the Castle during 1689. But famine throughout the country made a merger with its prosperous neighbour seem very attractive and the Scottish Parliament last sat in Edinburgh in 1707. The railway age took its first tentative steps by the Firth of Forth with the opening of the Tranent - Cockenzie waggonway in 1722, again with coal transport in mind. This became famous as the first railway to play a strategic role during a conflict when it was embroiled in the 1745 Battle of Prestonpans. The occasion was the last Jacobite rebellion aimed at restoring the exiled Stuarts to the throne, and Bonnie Prince Charlie was the instigator. Inevitably Edinburgh Castle suffered another siege, though this proved to be its last.

Following the gory and decisive Battle of Culloden, Scotland became peaceful after centuries of strife. A new spirit of optimism and national pride emerged and the Edinburgh area experienced an unprecedented growth of trade, industry and agriculture, whilst the city itself saw an incredible flourishing of arts, literature and philosophy. This manifested itself in material terms very evident today. During 1753 the Castle esplanade was created and this is now the site of the spectacular Military Tattoo. The elegant Royal Exchange (later the City Chambers) was built on the Royal Mile in 1761. Calton Hill gained its first building, the original observatory, during 1766 and the first part of the magnificent New Town, now the largest urban conservation area in

Now an integral yet proudly independent part of the city, Leith has been Edinburgh's seaport for centuries. It was also the goal for half a dozen local railway schemes. There is still plenty of cargo traffic through the docks and cruise ships still call, although other passenger business has faded away. On 29th August 1955 M.V. ST. NINIAN, owned by the North of Scotland, Orkney & Shetland Shipping Company, prepared to leave Leith for Aberdeen, Kirkwall and Lerwick. These weekly sailings were discontinued in 1971 when the company became part of P&O.

Edinburgh once had a very extensive tramway network which comprised more than 47 route miles at its maximum, operated by some 360 vehicles. With Princes Street providing a magnificent backdrop, car No.198 climbed away from The Mound on 29th August 1955. Flags were flying from the trolley rope for the annual Festival and the driver wore his white top summer uniform cap. In 1952 there was a drastic change in policy and the entire system was replaced by buses over the ensuing four years, routes 23 (Granton Road station - Morningside Road station) and 28 (Braids - Stanley Road) being the last to run on 16th November 1956.

Britain, was started during 1767. Connecting the Old and New Towns soon became a priority and North Bridge was built in 1772. The second crossing was much more curious. During the 1790s an Old Town tailor started to build a causeway for his New Town customers across the boggy floor of the recently drained Nor'Loch (which was originally created as

a medieval defence). Edinburgh Corporation took on The Mound project itself and when the embankment was completed thirty years later it had consumed two million cart loads of material from building work in the New Town! Meanwhile Leith was booming and the commercial area of Constitution Street and Bernard Street developed.

The one and three quarter mile Pinkie Railway from coal pits at Pinkie Hill, south east of Musselburgh, to the little harbour at Fisherrow, was opened in 1814. Another horse-operated waggonway with iron edge rails was the Edmonston Railway of 1818 which ran for less than four miles from Newton Colliery near Millerhill to Little France on the Dalkeith Road, south of Edinburgh. Calton Hill gained the Nelson Monument and a new observatory in 1816/18, the Radical Road round Arthur's Seat was constructed during 1820 as a kind of job creation scheme for unemployed weavers, and the proposed National Monument on Calton Hill was started during 1822. The residents of Princes Street secured a legal right to ban commercial development and retain their open vista of the Gardens and Castle opposite during 1827. A year earlier the Edinburgh & Dalkeith Railway was authorised and the bulk of this sophisticated horse-operated line opened in 1831, absorbing the Edmonston waggonway in the process.

There were hints of a fundamental change in transport thinking during 1832 when a passenger service began on the Edinburgh & Dalkeith and the Pinkie waggonway was abandoned. By this time The Mound had been completed and Calton Hill was festooned with monuments. Leith gained its much wanted independence from Edinburgh in 1833. The Railway Age proper came to the city during 1842 when the superbly engineered Edinburgh & Glasgow Railway reached

The North British Railway was a dominant influence in Edinburgh for nearly eighty years and its distinctive engines and carriages still operated several main line services in the late 1920s. Class D34 4-4-0 No.9281 GLEN MURRAN, in apple green, left Waverley for Glasgow Queen Street around 1928/29, before it was painted in black in common with other LNER small passenger locomotives. The train is passing Waverley West cabin which disappeared when the station was resignalled between 1936 and 1938, using colour lights controlled from a new concrete box off to the right. Photograph J.J. Cunningham.

Four of Edinburgh's main lines are still very active, with class 91 electrics coming in from London King's Cross, West Coast 87s and 90s appearing over the former Caledonian route from Carlisle, HSTs heading north to Aberdeen and pairs of 158s providing the half hourly shuttle to Glasgow. Tthere has also been a revival of local services - albeit very modest - with a few new stations, the reopening of the Bathgate line, electrification to North Berwick and a much improved timetable on the Fife Circle. On 6th June 1994 Sprinter 156 502 forming the 17.14 to Motherwell received passengers at Waverley's suburban island platform. These trains normally depart from the western bays, but prolonged signalling work at Haymarket meant that incoming workings had to run round the Suburban line via Morningside Road and thus approached from the east. The suburban station had hardly changed at all from the early 1900s and retains some delightful Edwardian ironwork. Photograph Paul Anderson.

Like London King's Cross, Edinburgh Waverley has always seen the latest and best East Coast motive power. Class A1 4-6-2 No.4472 FLYING SCOTSMAN, probably the best known Gresley Pacific of all, received last minute attention before departing with a southbound express around 1930. Photograph J.J. Cunningham.

Haymarket. Its terminus was in a classical style reminiscent of the New Town, but new public buildings in the spreading built-up area increasingly reflected Victorian taste, beginning with Donaldson's Hospital west of Haymarket. The demand for travel was increasing rapidly and the first part of the Edinburgh, Leith & Granton Railway - intended as a link from Princes Street to the Firth of Forth ferries - also opened in 1842. Two years later the North British Railway was authorised and services from Berwick upon Tweed to North Bridge commenced during 1846. At the same time the Edinburgh & Glasgow was extended through Princes Street Gardens to meet it, and a branch opened from Longniddry to the old county town of Haddington. None of these produced much in the way of worthwhile architecture, but 1846 also saw the completion of the Scott Monument. This spiky gothic spire rearing 200ft above Princes Street was designed, incredibly, by a local joiner! The Edinburgh & Dalkeith was absorbed and modified by the embryo North British and its spur to the little harbour at Fisherrow was used as a springing point for a branch to Musselburgh in 1847. This hectic period of railway construction was concluded by the opening of the Caledonian Railway from Carstairs to Lothian Road at the western end of Princes Street in 1848. It was fairly hectic on the streets as well, for Edinburgh was experiencing yet another period of civil unrest, this time due to food shortage. Just to add to the general hullabaloo, the traditional firing of the One o'clock Gun from the castle ramparts also began during 1848.

The next thirty years saw a substantial expansion of the railway network with new routes pushing out to Lothian and Borders towns, and other lines penetrating the coalfields and mill valleys. There was also a fair amount of jostling between the North British and Caledonian as they vied for traffic at Granton and Leith Docks. In 1849 branches opened to Hawick below the Cheviot Hills and Bathgate west of the city, whilst 1850 saw the completion of a modest single line from Drem to North Berwick. A very im-

Sadly, and perhaps unwisely in retrospect, Edinburgh was indifferent to its local railways. One by one, passenger services were withdrawn - with Leith losing its last trains to the city centre in 1962. The final departure from Leith North to Princes Street on 28th April was at 6.45pm, the usual two-car Gloucester railcar having been strengthened by a second set. However, the occasion attracted little public interest. Services on the Southside Suburban line ceased shortly afterwards and the Musselburgh and Corstorphine branches perished in due course.

portant event during the same year was the long-awaited opening of the Royal Border Bridge at Berwick upon Tweed, enabling through East Coast workings between Edinburgh and London to begin. Peebles was linked to the city by a heavily graded single track during 1855. Three years later one of the most touching episodes in Edinburgh's history unfolded. During 1858 a Skye Terrier known fondly as Greyfriars Bobby began a fourteen year vigil at the grave of his dead master, a local constable. At the One o'clock Gun he went to a nearby restaurant to be fed, and became a local celebrity. The statue erected to his memory in 1873 still stands in Candlemaker Row.

During 1860 the promenade at Portobello was completed, firmly establishing this small town as Edinburgh's own seaside resort, and from 1867 the young Robert Louis Stevenson spent his summers at a cottage in Swanston where he wrote about the nearby Pentland Hills. Meanwhile the railways were exploring new territory. A Caledonian branch from Slateford reached the harbour at Granton during 1861 and an extension began to serve Leith Docks in 1864. The Waverley route was established with the completion of the Hawick - Carlisle section in 1862, giving Edinburgh its fourth trunk route. A short but heavily engineered branch to Polton, serving important paper mills in the South Esk Valley, opened in 1867, whilst the line from Ratho to South Queensferry - anticipating a bridge

over the Firth of Forth - was finished in 1868. A new route from North Bridge station (by then known as Waverley) to Leith and Granton was opened by the North British during the same year in response to recent Caledonian advances. The Caley itself was eager to increase capacity and improve facilities at its main line terminus but ended up building another makeshift station at Princes Street in 1870, just a matter of yards from the Lothian Road site. A North British branch to Macmerry, east of Edinburgh, opened during 1872 with the aim of tapping an expanding coalfield, whilst an independent company built a difficult line to Penicuik serving mills alongside the South Esk, also in 1872. More tentacles to collieries and mills materialised, with the inauguration of a branch to Roslin and Loanhead above the South Esk Valley in 1874 and a contemporary Caledonian loop through Juniper Green and Balerno alongside the delightful Water of Leith. Caledonian passenger services from Princes Street to Leith commenced in 1879.

By then the railways around Edinburgh had a virtual monopoly of mineral traffic, carried most general goods, were a lifeline for many rural communities, and provided the only realistic means of long distance travel. However, the city itself was expanding rapidly and horse buses, then horse trams, attempted to fulfil local transport needs. Between the early 1880s and World War I both the North British and Caledonian made several moves to

capture suburban traffic, with varying degrees of success. In a wider context the companies were desperate to prove their superiority when it came to Anglo-Scottish traffic and this competition reached theatrical proportions with the 'Railway Races to the North'. There was a lot of money about in the railway industry, together with confidence, indeed a certain amount of arrogance. Engineering works in the Edinburgh area clearly reflected this, and some grandiose architecture emerged as well. In marked contrast certain rural areas away from the existing routes gained charming branch lines with lots of character but a limited future, as it turned out.

A few local stations opened over the years on North British lines north of the city centre, but the South Side Suburban route between Haymarket and the old Edinburgh & Dalkeith alignment at Duddingston, opened in 1884, was a determined attempt to serve the streets of tenements and villas spreading out from the Old Town. These developments were inevitably eclipsed by the legendary Forth Bridge, connecting Edinburgh and the south with Fife and the north, completed during 1890. Large scale railway projects were becoming commonplace by now, and a massive reconstruction of Waverley station began in 1892, accompanied by the quadrupling of tracks and tunnels west to Saughton Junction where the Forth Bridge line veered off. North Bridge, the first link between the Old Town and New

Sparkling Fairburn 2-6-4T No. 42273 with equally smart ex-LMS non-corridor stock terminated at Kingdknowe on 29th February 1964. The train was the 12.57pm from Edinburgh Princes Street. This outer surburban station closed four months later but reopened in 1971.

Town, was rebuilt during 1897 in connection with these works, the North British subscribing a third of the cost. The wealthy Caledonian Railway was shamed into doing something about its pathetic terminus as a result of this investment by its rival, and a highly ornate red sandstone building was erected at the western end of Princes Street in 1894. In the same year the Caley opened a branch to the developing suburb of Barnton. As the century which had established most of Edinburgh's railway network drew to a close, another speculative branch opened to Gullane on the sand hills west of North Berwick during 1898.

The reconstruction of Waverley station was completed in 1900, the massive North British Hotel opening alongside it during 1902, and the splendid Caledonian Hotel at the opposite end of Princes Street welcomed its first guests in 1903. Meanwhile an extremely rural branch had ventured out to Gifford in the shadow of the Lammermuir Hills some sixteen miles east of Edinburgh, optimistically wooing its first commuters during 1901. The Caledonian had been contemplating a far more ambitious local scheme for some time, involving a circular service from Princes Street to Newhaven, Leith and the east end, then back to the terminus. It would have included a long tunnel be-

low the city centre, but this was rejected and only the elevated Newhaven - Seafield section emerged, opening in 1903. The same year also saw the completion of a short North British branch to a huge terminus at Leith Central.

By the beginning of the 20th century the centres of most British cities had been largely rebuilt by the Victorians, Glasgow being a prime example. Edinburgh was an exception. The Old Town and New Town were under the care of commissioners and were too precious to be tampered with. There were some large Edwardian buildings in the heart of the capital, notably the two railway hotels on Princes Street, but most other grand edifices of the period were confined to the periphery. The Usher Hall of 1913 and St. Mary's Cathedral, completed in 1917, were examples. One final piece of railway infrastructure came into use during 1915. This was the Lothian Lines system near Niddrie, designed to improve coal transport from pits south east of the city to Leith Docks.

In the 1920s a long decline of local services began, initially as a result of bus competition in the hinterland and the electrification of Edinburgh's tramways. The Grouping of 1923 saw the North British passing to the London & North Eastern Railway (LNER) and the Caledonian ab-

sorbed by the London Midland & Scottish Railway (LMS). Apart from the withdrawal of South Leith - Portobello trains in 1905 and the permanent closure of Powderhall station at the beginning of 1917, the first casualties were the Granton and Macmerry passenger services in 1925, the latter an easy target for Scottish Motor Traction buses. Gullane branch trains ceased in 1932, followed by those to Gifford and Glencorse in 1933. The same decade saw a modest fightback with the opening of new halts at Balgreen (1934), East Pilton (1934) and House o'Hill (1937) on the Corstorphine, Leith North and Barnton lines respectively. Closures during World War II were relatively rare, yet Edinburgh experienced two of them. The short Dalkeith branch lost its passenger trains in 1942 and the Balerno loop was denied services from 1943. Just over six months before the LNER and LMS became part of British Railways, on 1st January 1948, the antiquated North Leith terminus became goods only. At least the town retained alternative services, unlike Haddington which became isolated from the passenger network in 1949. Meanwhile the city itself was about to become the major tourist attraction it remains today, with the launch of the Edinburgh International Festival of Music and Drama in 1947.

BR continued the rationalisation by ending passenger services from Waverley to Polton and Penicuik in 1951, abandoning Barnton during the same year, and closing the huge Leith Central terminus in 1952. Thus far, the network remained intact and most lines still dealt with goods traffic. The infamous 1960s changed all that, largely as a result of the Beeching 'reshaping', and an avalanche of closures came in just seven years. During spring 1962 Leith lost its last passenger trains when the former Caledonian branch from Princes Street succumbed, preceded by the withdrawal of services on the former North British branch to Peebles and followed by the end of trains on the once busy Suburban circle. Some of the complex network of former Caley lines west of Princes Street station was abandoned in 1964 and local services from Waverley to Portobello and Musselburgh perished shortly afterwards. Princes Street terminus itself closed in 1965. Following this mayhem, the need for further closures began to be questioned, and the end of the Corstorphine branch and Waverley route in 1967 and 1969 respectively was surrounded by controversy. Although Edinburgh's main line services were as comprehensive as ever, few British cities had had a once wide ranging local railway network hacked away so ruthlessly. Fortunately there has since been a positive side to the story, with several new or reopened stations - Kingsknowe (1971), South Gyle (1985), Wester Hailes (1987), Curriehill (1987), Musselburgh (1988) and Wallyford (1994).

It would be a shame to end this introduction with a tale of decline. The following pages examine Edinburgh's railways in happier days and to set the scene an extract from the notebook of W.A.C. Smith for Friday 24th August 1945 has been included. This was the traffic observed at the west end of Waverley station between 12.30pm and 2.00pm:

'The first departure was the five coach 12.35pm to Corstorphine headed by V1 No.465 and five minutes later the first arrival brought un-named A2/1 No.3699 on the 11.20am from Glasgow Queen Street due at 12.37pm and comprising eight corridor coaches strengthened by three non-corridors, including a clerestory-roofed vehicle, plus a six-wheel passenger brake van. A couple of minutes later an NB 'Scott' went off with the 12.28pm suburban inner circle working from Leith Central, and V1 No.2924 came in with the 12.12pm from Leith Central via the outer circle. Meanwhile the 8.50am from Aberdeen, twelve vehicles, had arrived two minutes late at 12.47pm hauled by V2 No.4865. The next departure should have been the 12.45pm from Leith Central to Glasgow Queen Street leaving Waverley at 1.00pm and one of the fastest trains of the day between the two cities in 68 minutes, but it was 1.06pm before this, a D11 with eleven corridors plus a passenger brake and Southern Railway utility van, got away following another D11 (No.6386 LORD GLENALLAN) on the 1.04pm to Corstorphine. The 1.09pm for Dundee Tay Bridge departed on time and had D49 No.2753 CHESHIRE on six corridors, two non-corridors and two vans. A V1 then went out on the 12.58pm Leith Central to Duddingston and the 1.00pm from Corstorphine arrived behind D33 ex-North British 'Intermediate' 4-4-0 No.9332. Similar (though, in fact, class D32) No.9893 arrived on the four coach 11.56am from Thornton Junction via Dunfermline while a couple of minutes later sister engine No.9886 left on the 1.16pm to Crail and D34 No.9291 GLEN QUOICH arrived at 1.28pm with the 12.04pm from Thornton Junction via Kirkcaldy. The next departure was at 1.30pm to Stirling via Alloa with V1 No.402 heading a horsebox, five non-corridor coaches, an LMS passenger brake and two goods vans. The 1.30pm inner circle from Leith Central had the unidentified ex-North British 4-4-0 seen earlier in charge and the 1.13pm outer circle was powered by V1 No.2924 making its second trip round the 'Sub'. Another of the class, No.465, arrived back from Corstorphine with the 1.33pm. The last departure seen was the 8.45am from York to Glasgow Queen Street, punctual at 2.00pm with V2 No.4807 on thirteen coaches. During the hour and a half there had been numerous shunting movements by the J83 pilots, eighteen light engine workings to and from Haymarket loco shed, including the extravagantly named V2 No.4780 THE SNAPPER, THE EAST YORKSHIRE REGIMENT - THE DUKE OF YORK'S OWN and a solitary down freight hauled by a J37 0-6-0.'

Elderly North British goods engines survived in the Edinburgh area almost until the end of steam. Snowplough fitted J36 0-6-0 No. 65334 plodded along the main line between Monktonhall and Niddrie with a loaded coal train on 3rd April 1961. The new connection from Millerhill Yard is in the foreground.

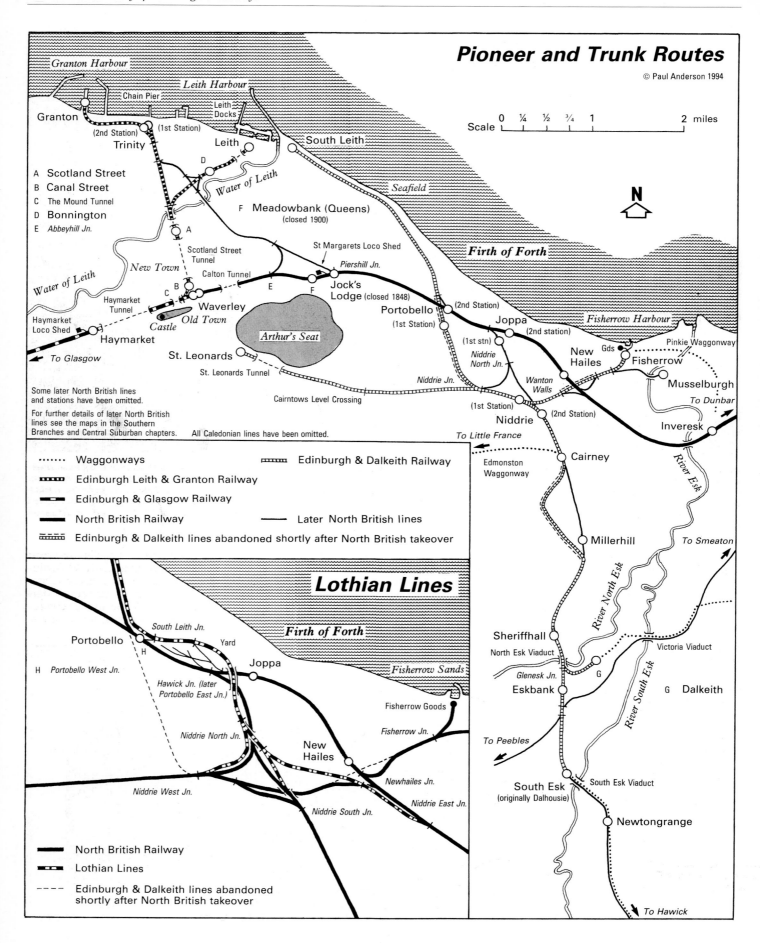

Pioneer and Trunk Routes

© Paul Anderson 1994

Scale 0 ¼ ½ ¾ 1 2 miles

A Scotland Street
B Canal Street
C The Mound Tunnel
D Bonnington
E *Abbeyhill Jn.*

Granton Harbour
Chain Pier
Leith Harbour
Leith Docks
Granton
(2nd Station) (1st Station)
Trinity Leith
South Leith
Seafield
Firth of Forth
F Meadowbank (Queens)
(closed 1900)
St Margarets Loco Shed
Water of Leith
New Town
Scotland Street Tunnel
Calton Tunnel
Piershill Jn.
Water of Leith
Haymarket Tunnel
Haymarket Loco Shed
Castle Old Town
Waverley
Jock's Lodge (closed 1848)
Portobello
(1st Station)
(2nd Station)
Joppa
(2nd station)
Fisherrow Harbour
Pinkie Waggonway
Haymarket
To Glasgow
St. Leonards
Arthur's Seat
St. Leonards Tunnel
Cairntows Level Crossing
Niddrie Jn.
Niddrie North Jn.
Wanton Walls
New Hailes
Gds
Fisherrow
Musselburgh
To Dunbar
(1st stn)
(1st Station)
(2nd Station)
Niddrie
Inveresk
To Little France
Edmonston Waggonway
Cairney
River Esk
To Smeaton

Some later North British lines and stations have been omitted.

For further details of later North British lines see the maps in the Southern Branches and Central Suburban chapters. All Caledonian lines have been omitted.

Millerhill

······ Waggonways
▭▭▭ Edinburgh & Dalkeith Railway
▰▰▰ Edinburgh Leith & Granton Railway
▬▬▬ Edinburgh & Glasgow Railway
━━━ North British Railway
───── Later North British lines
▥▥▥ Edinburgh & Dalkeith lines abandoned shortly after North British takeover

Lothian Lines

South Leith Jn.
Portobello
H
Yard
Firth of Forth
Joppa
H *Portobello West Jn.*
Hawick Jn. (later Portobello East Jn.)
Fisherrow Sands
Niddrie North Jn.
Fisherrow Goods
Fisherrow Jn.
New Hailes
Niddrie West Jn.
Newhailes Jn.
Niddrie East Jn.
Niddrie South Jn.

Sheriffhall
North Esk Viaduct
Victoria Viaduct
Glenesk Jn.
G
Eskbank
G Dalkeith
River North Esk
River South Esk
To Peebles
South Esk
(originally Dalhousie)
South Esk Viaduct
Newtongrange
To Hawick

━━━ North British Railway
▰▰▰ Lothian Lines
───── Edinburgh & Dalkeith lines abandoned shortly after North British takeover

Chapter One
The Pioneers

St. Leonards terminus occupied an extensive site on the southern edge of the Old Town and it was laid out for mineral traffic, numerous sidings fanning out to individual coal banks. A row of grim warehouses grew up on the eastern side and it must have been a rather unappealing setting for the passenger services which ran from 1832 to 1847 and briefly reappeared during 1860. The primitive platform canopy can be seen above J35 0-6-0 No.64570 which stood at St Leonards with the 'Edinburgh & Dalkeith' railtour on 25th August 1962. The figure second from left in the group in the foreground is W.A.C. Smith who, as Scottish Secretary of the Stephenson Locomotive Society, organised the tour. Photograph W.S. Sellar.

Before Edinburgh was linked to England by rail and the pattern of trunk routes serving the Scottish capital became firmly established, two local lines with contrasting ambitions were constructed. Both of them included substantial engineering works and operated passenger services. Eventually they became enmeshed in the overall network and were modified, extended and otherwise adapted to meet changing needs. Somewhat remarkably, most of this early railway mileage survived in one form or another until fairly recently.

The Edinburgh & Dalkeith was a very early scheme and a contemporary of pioneering local projects elsewhere in Great Britain, including the Garnkirk & Glasgow and Dundee & Newtyle. Its prime purpose was to carry coal from the Lothian coalfield to the hungry hearths of 'Auld Reekie', a duty the company performed admirably for over fourteen years. Branches were thrust out to the quays of Fisherrow, the docks at Leith and Dalkeith town centre, resulting in an impressive route of nearly fourteen miles. However, motive power was less adventurous and the Edinburgh & Dalkeith

remained horse operated throughout its independent existence. Its well known pseudonym 'The Innocent Railway' began with a comment about the company's resilience to change, but gave rise to a legend that nobody was ever injured on the

line - which was somewhat divorced from reality. The Edinburgh, Leith & Newhaven came later and was conceived at a time when the great trunk routes were being planned. This little line to the sea was also quite far sighted, for it saw it-

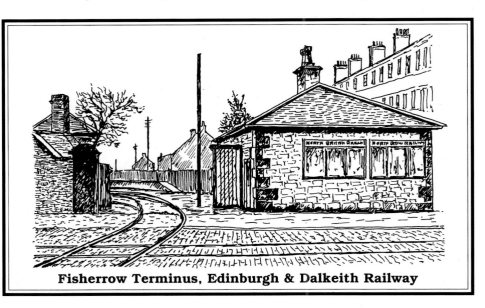

Fisherrow Terminus, Edinburgh & Dalkeith Railway

self as a link between the city centre and the ferries to Fife and further afield. After a change of name to Edinburgh, Leith & Granton, and a hesitant start, the company achieved its ambition and was soon taken over by a larger concern poised to control the potentially lucrative rail traffic from Edinburgh to Perth and Dundee. It took the mighty Forth Bridge to reduce the local line to a modest suburban role.

EDINBURGH & DALKEITH

Vibrant and prosperous it may have been, but in the early 1800s Edinburgh could not satisfy its voracious appetite for coal. The Union Canal struggled to bring sufficient supplies from the west and coastal colliers were subject to the whims of the North Sea. There were pits at Dalhousie, Newbattle and Carberry barely six miles south east of the Old Town, yet carts often became bogged down in winter and suffered broken axles in summer on the rutted roads. Furthermore, carriers were notoriously corrupt and this added to the general frustration. Solutions had been sought for some time before a meeting convened in Edinburgh during 1824 decided to press ahead with a railway to the nearby coalfield. It had the support of no less than ten aristocratic landowners, including some with Lothian mining interests. With virtually no opposition the Edinburgh & Dalkeith Railway was authorised on 26th May 1826 and subsequent Acts in 1829 and 1834 sanctioned various branches.

The main line ran for eight and a quarter miles from a goods yard at St.

On 12th August 1961 J35 0-6-0 No.64479 ambled across Cairntous level crossing, just west of Duddingston, with empty mineral wagons from St. Leonards. Arthur's Seat and Salisbury Crags rear up on the right, whilst the Old Town forms the distant skyline. Four youngsters, in time-honoured fashion, have clambered up the gates to wave at the train, although the smallest one seems about to lose his grip! The crew peer down benevolently. This delightful view is a picture of innocence and order, which seem to be sadly lacking nowadays, and this section of the 'Innocent Railway' is now a footpath. Photograph W.S. Sellar.

Leonards, in the shadow of Salisbury Crags, via Niddrie, Craighall, Millerhill and Eskbank to a terminus at Dalhousie Mains, above the South Esk near Dalkeith. Its opening as far as the nearest colliery at Craighall was celebrated on 4th July 1831 and the remainder came into use with little publicity during the following October. The 4ft 6in gauge double track consisted of fish bellied iron rails fixed to sandstone blocks with hard whinstone chippings as ballast, and stone walls or hedges bordered the right of way. Coal traffic was worked by contractor's horses and wagons, an arrangement already familiar on earlier lines.

St. Leonards depot occupied eight acres of land near Newington, just beyond the existing built-up area of the city and about a mile from the Castle. Eventually numerous sidings fanned out on the south side and a range of rather grim warehouses and workshops faced them, below the towering bulk of Salisbury Crags. Immediately east of St. Leonards an abrupt spur thrusting out from Arthur,s Seat demanded a tunnel 572 yards long and 20ft wide. The interior was lined with fine stonework and 25 gas lamps provided illumination - as was often the case with such pioneering projects. East of Newington the ground fell away sharply towards a low plain around Duddingston and the Edinburgh & Dalkeith was obliged to fall at 1 in 30 for 1,170 yards from its St. Leonards terminus, including the tunnel section. This gradient was clearly beyond the resources of horse traction, so the incline was worked by rope, powered by two stationary steam engines featuring cylinders with 28in bore and 78in stroke, working at a pressure of 5lb per square inch. Colliery waste was used as fuel and the stoker was provided with a company house. Drums 11ft in diameter accommodated the two 5in circumference ropes, each weighing 37cwt, and these were guided by 2ft diameter rollers located between the rails at 8 yard intervals. Loads up to 30 tons could be winched

By 1838 the four arms of the Edinburgh & Dalkeith system met at Niddrie, and despite a massive expansion of rail facilities there was still evidence of the Innocent Railway a century and a quarter later as A1 Pacific No.60147 NORTH EASTERN passed Niddrie West Junction with empty coaching stock, on 16th July 1962. Arthur's Seat dominated the skyline and the houses of Bingham Park stretched away beyond Duddingston Park Road in the middle distance. In front of them the low embankment identified the original route to South Leith which was abandoned in 1849. It has since disappeared, along with the field in the foreground, now occupied by a new estate. Back in 1962, there was an extensive yard to the left, the connection with the North British main line was immediately to the right of the engine, and a Lothian Lines spur climbed away near the telegraph poles. The train is using the E&D St. Leonards - South Esk alignment.

South east of Niddrie the Edinburgh & Dalkeith was transformed into a main line as well as an important coal artery. Seen from Whitehill Road bridge, A3 Pacific No.60093 CORONACH stormed towards the Southern Uplands with the 5.52pm express from Edinburgh Waverley to Carlisle on 3rd April 1961. The site of Niddrie's second station was in the background. On the left, sidings served Monktonhall Colliery - still open in 1994 under private ownership. To the right, Millerhill Yard was under construction. With the virtual disappearance of freight traffic the remaining sidings see little use, although there is an engineers' yard and the diesel depot still services locos - including the occasional visiting steam engine. The land once occupied by Newcraighall Colliery on the extreme left now accommodates a complex known as Mega Bowl.

in by the stationary engines whilst descending trains used gravity, drawing the rope out as they went.

The track continued through open country past Duddingston Loch and the Bonnie Wells O' Wearie to the tiny hamlet of Niddrie which soon became a junction and the focus of the E&D network. At Craighall the main line turned south towards Millerhill then skirted the wooded grounds of Dalkeith Palace. Lothian's principal pits were almost in sight, but the terrain ahead did not favour railway construction, especially at such an early date. The North Esk, tumbling down from the Pentland Hills and the South Esk, draining the Moorfoot Hills, met just north of Dalkeith, having carved deep clefts in the plateau around Bonnyrigg and Newbattle. A substantial bridge 60ft above the North Esk was needed to push the rails on to Eskbank, Hardengreen and Dalhousie overlooking the formidable South Esk Gorge. But with Edinburgh desperate for coal and the wealthy mine owners eager to provide it, the prompt and very expensive mile and a half extension to Arniston was understandable. The Marquis of Lothian financed the line and it incorporated a huge bridge across the South Esk with sandstone piers supporting a timber superstructure for nearly 340 yards. It opened on 21st January 1832 and an increasing number of coal trains rattled across the valley.

Fisherrow, where there was a harbour for nearby Musselburgh, soon claimed the

attention of the Edinburgh & Dalkeith and a mile and a half branch from Niddrie opened in October 1831. It descended at 1 in 52 past Brunstane and Wanton Walls, followed the east side of Newhailes Road then slipped down to Fisherrow Quays across New Street. When passenger services began, the line became popular with local fishwives who travelled in open carriages to Edinburgh where they sold their wares shouting 'caller haddie, partan, ou' (fresh haddock, crab, oyster). Leith was also a desirable goal and was reached during 1838 by a three and a half mile branch from Niddrie. The line curved northwards from the junction on an embankment and soon crossed the Niddrie - Portobello Road on the level. It continued along the west side of the road as far as Friggate Burn and having bridged this lit-

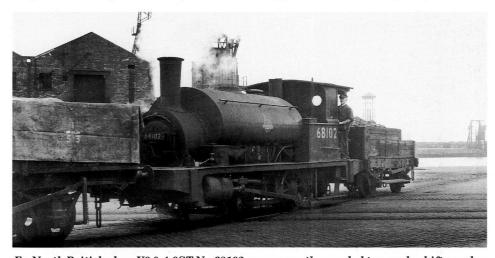

Ex-North British class Y9 0-4-0ST No.68102, permanently coupled to a makeshift wooden tender, shunted sidings deep in the Leith Docks complex on 29th August 1955. Its driver proffered a wry smile, but his working conditions would probably not be tolerated today. Spanish esparto grass for use in local paper mills was most likely contained in the sheeted wagon, whilst drops for shipment coal from the Lothians punctuated the skyline. Leith Docks underwent a massive expansion during the Railway Age, the succession of new basins being Victoria (1851), Albert (1869), Edinburgh (1881) and Imperial (1903). Industries such as sugar refining and glass making also developed.

Just over a mile east of Leith the Edinburgh & Dalkeith crossed Seafield Road on the level, but eventually a bridge was installed. On 15th October 1960, J36 0-6-0 No.65288 emerged from beneath Seafield Road and briskly passed Meadows signal box with a lengthy freight from South Leith yard. The lines behind the cabin led to extensive sidings and the track on the embankment was a connection from the Caledonian's Seafield extension. Eastern General Hospital is prominent on the skyline.

Ex-North British J35 0-6-0 No.64510, the last active member of the class, prepared to propel the afternoon freight away from Dalkeith towards Hardengreen yard on 24th May 1962. On this occasion the trip working was quite well loaded.

tle stream, descended at 1 in 69 towards the sea. At Westbank the line passed beneath the Edinburgh - Portobello road and crossed Craigentinny Meadows. Beyond here it assumed a course along the landward side of Seafield Road where horses and drivers alike were frequently subjected to salt spray and the ravages of North Sea gales during the winter. No doubt Leith's Constitution Street terminus came as a welcome relief in such conditions. The final Edinburgh & Dalkeith extension was a modest half mile branch from Glenesk Junction to the centre of

Dalkeith. It opened in autumn 1839 and a lengthy private line continued to the Duke of Buccleuch's collieries at Smeaton and Cowden, across another substantial viaduct over the South Esk.

The Edinburgh & Dalkeith more than fulfilled its promise to supply coal and became a valued city amenity. Some 2,000 tons of fuel a week were soon trundling into St. Leonards, and exports were possible once the Leith branch opened. In addition, one of the more adventurous contractors converted a stagecoach for railway use and began a passenger run

from South Esk to St. Leonards on 2nd June 1832. Its popularity took nearly everyone by surprise and passenger numbers were soon averaging 800 per day. This encouraged the E&D to start its own service during 1834 and the railway took over completely in 1836. Once the Leith and Dalkeith branches opened, Niddrie became an interchange of some significance, with the hourly main line service dropping and collecting carriages for Leith and Fisherrow. By 1840 the E&D owned about 40 passenger coaches - some enclosed with three compartments, others basically open trucks with benches. It was a colourful operation with the guard on his lofty seat blowing a bugle at frequent intervals and the trains stopping anywhere to collect passengers. No tickets were issued and apparently the conductors often had difficulty collecting fares as people refused to say where they were going! At one time, early morning bathers' specials were run from St. Leonards to Portobello and private carriages could be hired at any time of the day or night.

Inevitably the local concern could not continue in this manner, faced with the rising tide of railway construction nationally. Its strategic access to docks and mines made it a desirable acquisition for the embryo North British Railway and despite protests the larger company was authorised to take over the Edinburgh & Dalkeith on 21st July 1845. The North British paid out £113,000 compared with the £130,000 used to build the system. The same Act sanctioned conversion of the E&D to standard gauge, permitted the use of steam engines (except to Leith) and allowed the North British to proceed with a branch from Edinburgh to Hawick employing part of the alignment to South Esk. Work started on re-gauging and laying sleepered track in 1846, but because of the demand a two-hourly passenger service was more or less maintained over the former E&D until June 1847. Locomotives began working from St. Leonards to Niddrie on 15th February 1847, the winding engines having been consigned to the scrapyard. Steam hauled services to Dalkeith from St. Leonards and the North British General station (later Waverley) commenced on 14th July 1847, along with those from General to Gorebridge on the uncompleted Hawick line. St. Leonards had become something of a lost cause for passenger traffic by this time and facilities were withdrawn on 1st November 1847, though there was still a long career ahead of it as a goods depot.

The rest of the Edinburgh & Dalkeith system underwent a certain amount of surgery to mould it into the North British network. Fisherrow received early attention following an Act of 26th June 1846. Where the old alignment intersected the new main line, a sweeping spur was built to give direct access to Edinburgh General, and a shorter link permit-

Musselburgh terminus boasted an attractive stone building facing a large forecourt at the junction of Inveresk Road and Station Road. It was in the fashionable Tudor style and featured authentic details such as angular dripstones above the windows and a porch with decorative battlements and a fine entrance arch. The photograph was taken on 29th August 1964 just a week before passenger services were withdrawn, but cheap day tickets to Edinburgh for 1s 1d were still being promoted on the noticeboards. Goods traffic lasted for another six years. Subsequently nearly all traces of the railway at Musselburgh were swept away and the trackbed was replaced by a new highway, Olivebank Road.

ted through traffic between St. Leonards and the coast route. Between their respective junctions at Newhailes and Wanton Walls the E&D track was abandoned. At the same time a half mile branch was built from the Fisherrow line across a skew bridge spanning the River Esk to a well appointed terminus convenient for Musselburgh High Street. It opened on 16th July 1847, leaving the Fisherrow stub to deal with goods traffic alone. Also in 1847, a short spur above the Friggate Burn was authorised so that South Leith passenger trains could run into a separate platform at the new Portobello main line station, thus affording more direct connections with Edinburgh. This opened in summer 1849 and the former E&D Portobello station nearby closed, along with the original route to Niddrie. The South Leith line closed on 9th October 1856 for doubling and reconstruction, eventually reopening with steam traction during 1858. The Hawick branch left the

Driver J. Wood of St. Margarets shed posed with V1 2-6-2T No.67668 at Musselburgh prior to working the 6.29pm to Edinburgh Waverley on 21st May 1955. After patiently listening to his views on pay differentials just a week before the notorious ASLEF strike, the photographer was rewarded with a footplate trip to Portobello! The terminus had a fine overall roof and broad side platforms with a central track for releasing engines. Ample goods facilities including a large shed were provided, and by this time the western side of the passenger station had become an extension of the yard, the end screen cut away to assist vehicle access.

At Newhailes Junction the Musselburgh branch joined the North British Edinburgh - Berwick tracks, again by a sharp curve requiring check rails. A Gloucester set forming the 1.21pm departure for Waverley passed this deceptively rural location and gained access to the East Coast main line on 3rd April 1961. The original Fisherrow alignment ran at right angles behind this viewpoint from Newcraighall Road bridge, whilst the 1847 connection from the North British route to St. Leonards could be identified by a low bank behind the B1 and J35 attending rakes of empty coaching stock. A Lothian Lines spur occupied the high embankment.

Edinburgh - Berwick main line at Hawick Junction, later Portobello East Junction, and joined the former E&D at Niddrie South Junction. A spur from Niddrie North Junction to Niddrie West Junction (virtually the old interchange point in E&D days) gave access to St. Leonards. The old horse line was employed as far as South Esk but it was new construction beyond there, into the Southern Uplands.

In 1862 the Hawick line became part of the Waverley route to Carlisle and with the opening of branches to Peebles, Dolphinton, Polton, Penicuik and Glencorse, the southern limb of the Edinburgh & Dalkeith became a busy corridor for both long distance and suburban trains. Individual stations experienced mixed fortunes. A second Niddrie station was built at what is now New Craighall to replace the nearby E&D facilities and permit Hawick trains to call, but it only lasted until 1st February 1869. Millerhill opened on 20th February 1849 and survived until 7th November 1955. Eskbank & Dalkeith (Eskbank until January 1954) closed along with the Waverley route on 6th January 1969. South Esk (Dalhousie until July 1847) was replaced by Newtongrange on the opposite side of the river on 1st August 1908, and this also succumbed with the Carlisle line. Regular passenger services were withdrawn from Dalkeith terminus on 5th January 1942, though freight lasted until 10th August 1964. The various suburban and rural branch passenger services feeding

the old E&D route all perished before the Waverley route, but coal remained important and Millerhill Yard was opened on 18th June 1962 to centralise marshalling

activities. With the drastic decline of mining since the 1960s even this traffic was progressively whittled away.

Returning to earlier years, there was a rather peculiar development at St. Leonards. In a brave attempt to raise its status, passenger services to Dalkeith, Portobello and Leith were reinstated on 1st June 1860 but the station was as inconvenient as ever - even for the Old Town - and the experiment ceased after just four months, on 30th September. Local breweries and bonded warehouses continued to provide traffic and coal was unloaded until 22nd July 1968. South Leith lost its passenger shuttle from Portobello on 2nd January 1905, having been largely eclipsed by the branch to Leith Central which had opened eighteen months previously and also received suburban trains calling at Portobello. Most of the line to South Leith is still open for freight. Although workings to Fisherrow harbour ceased long ago, the branch was retained for goods traffic and closed as late as 2nd October 1961, latterly serving a solitary coal merchant. The Musselburgh passenger trains finished on 7th September 1964 and public goods facilities followed on 7th December 1970, with private sidings lasting for a short while.

EDINBURGH, LEITH & GRANTON

Edinburgh's shoreline, roughly two and a half miles from the Old Town, extends from Granton in the west to Leith in the east. For two thousand years this four

The second Trinity station was a truly delightful building in smooth grey stone, wholly in harmony with its views of the Firth of Forth, hilly Inchkeith island and the distant Fife hills which often present grey hues themselves. A solid two storey facade, with simple square windows and continuous roof line, faced the steep approach from Trinity Crescent whilst the single storey platform elevation incorporated twin gables featuring bay windows enlivened by decorative hoods. In summer 1914 the station had twelve trains each way between Granton and Edinburgh Waverley and was very popular with Newhaven fishwives travelling to the city. With a short, sharp 1 in 100 climb from the shoreline, southbound trains approached the platforms in a lively fashion. By 7th April 1958 when the photograph was taken, the former railway premises had become a house and remains so today. The original terminus was off to the left, approached past the retaining wall below York Road in the distance. It closed as a goods yard on 2nd November 1925.

Granton was once a major focus of road, rail and water transport. The station and ferry berth stood on Middle Pier (in the background) but they were hidden from the view of passengers by the corner of the Customs and Excise building in this 3rd September 1955 panorama. Western Breakwater is in the background with a collier berthed alongside it, and a row of rail-mounted grab cranes are silhouetted against the misty Firth of Forth and Fife's hilly coastline. Granton Square was once the terminus of seven tram services, and domed-roof standard car No.226 waited to leave on route 14. One of Edinburgh Corporation's strange open rear platform Leyland single deckers and a taxi firm in the corner of the square completed the public transport miscellany. Much of the western harbour has since been filled in and is occupied by commercial premises, whilst the eastern haven is now a marina.

1700s there were ships plying to Scandinavia, Russia, North America and the West Indies, with imports ranging from timber to tar and rum to rice. Handsome modern buildings and a fine stone pier reflected this prosperous trade. Ship-building developed as well, and the SIRIUS launched in 1837, was the first steam vessel to cross the Atlantic. Always staunchly independent, even today, Leith has resisted the municipal influence of Edinburgh since medieval times. After years of wrangling it became a separate borough in 1838 only to be absorbed again by the city in 1920. Newhaven grew up as a modest fishing village about a mile west of Leith and remained largely oblivious to the political events and burgeoning trade affecting its near neighbour. However, it did have a brief spell of glory in the early 16th century. James IV, at war with England, was desperate to build up the Scottish navy and constructed his fleet there. The yard's finest product was GREAT MICHAEL, a magnificent fighting vessel launched in 1511 as the Scottish flagship. With the King's death at the Battle of Flodden, Scotland's naval ambitions collapsed and Newhaven reverted to a prosaic fishing community. Oysters became a speciality, until overfished to extinction by the early 1800s, but herrings remained important, and Newhaven fishwives in their particularly colourful attire traded their wares around Edinburgh until quite recently.

mile stretch of the Firth of Forth has supported communities gleaning a living from various activities associated with the sea, although the nearby city has always influenced virtually every stage of their development. Leith grew up on both banks of the Water of Leith where it joined the estuary. The harbour became important in medieval times for exporting salted fish and importing Bordeaux wine, but general trade grew and for centuries Leith was Scotland's chief port. In 1636 the town was described as 'a pretty little haven' with neat wooden piers, poor stone houses, and an expanse of cornfields separating it from Edinburgh. By the late

Strung along the Firth of Forth were several little passenger piers with sailings to Fife, Dundee, Aberdeen and distant harbours in England. The vessels were

Eventually Granton Harbour boasted a pier 1,700 ft long by 180 ft wide with ten jetties, two low water slips, eleven warehouses and sixteen cranes. Great breakwaters to the east and west enclosed 130 acres of water whilst iron foundries, bonded warehouses, a shipbuilding complex and a vast timber yard developed on the shoreline. The North British had a network of sidings in the area and the Caledonian approached from the west. A connection between the two systems crossed Harbour Road and this was being shunted by J88 0-6-0T No.68325 on 7th April 1958 as Edinburgh Corporation double-decker No.931 waited in Granton Square. The engine was shedded at St. Margarets and most other classes from 64A were seen at Granton at one time or another. Until the Slateford - Craiglockhart connection was put in by BR, this was the main freight transfer point between the LMS and LNER systems in Edinburgh. Mineral wagons in the background occupied the original EL&G alignment on to the pier. The course of the connecting line and even a length of rails across the road were still visible in 1994.

small sailing packets and connections were provided by stagecoaches renowned for irregularity and unpunctuality. Sir Walter Scott in one of his novels vividly described the frustration involved in attempting such a journey. Remonstrations about an interminable delay took place at the coach office in Edinburgh, followed by a dilatory journey during which a spring broke and the horse cast a shoe. Progress was likened to that of a fly through a glue pot, and clearly there was need for something better. A meeting held during 1835 to discuss the problem resulted in the Edinburgh, Leith & Newhaven Railway which obtained its Act of Parliament on 13th August 1836. It was to consist of a two and a quarter mile line from Princes Street Gardens to the shore at Newhaven, with a mile and a quarter branch to Leith, leaving the main line a mile or so out of the city terminus. A substantial tunnel was planned under the New Town. Construction costs were estimated at £100,000 and a 15% dividend was forecast, although constant reminders of this potential bonanza perhaps betrayed the proprietors' underlying uncertainty. The Edinburgh, Leith & Newhaven did not get off to a good start. Financial experts expressed doubts about the viability of the scheme, engineering problems emerged with the Leith branch, and difficult landowners in the New Town landed the company with prolonged and costly litigation.

Within three years there were plans for a new harbour at Trinity, on the Granton side of Newhaven, and by an Act of 1st July 1839 the original scheme was abandoned in favour of a line slightly further west, although the tunnel alignment from Canal Street was to remain unchanged. At long last, on 31st August 1842, the one and a quarter miles of track from Scotland Street to Trinity opened for traffic. Its southern terminus, in the area known as Canonmills, occupied a cramped site below steeply sloping ground at the eastern end of Royal Crescent. Almost immediately the rails passed beneath Rodney Street by a short tunnel faced in very fine stonework. The line continued northwards across the Water of Leith and entered a broad cutting through rising ground on the opposite bank. Beyond Warriston and Ferry Road a severe rock cutting and another short tunnel, below East Trinity Road, were required. The northern terminus overlooked the shore from an elevated site on the opposite side of Starbank Road and was a short walk from the curious Chain Pier, served by sailing vessels to Fife. Steam traction was planned but the engines were never ordered and horses had considerable difficulty coping with the carriages intended for them. Lighter stock was eventually acquired. Furthermore, Scotland Street was remote from the city centre and horse buses provided debilitating competition.

It was not a very auspicious beginning.

Back in 1834, there was a proposal to create new harbour facilities at Granton, just west of Trinity. The landowner with foreshore rights was the Duke of Buccleuch who, convinced of the significance of the project, decided to have it built at his own expense. Work began in October 1837 and the first part opened on 28th June 1838, Coronation Day, was named Victoria Jetty in honour of the Queen. Sailing boats to Burntisland commenced immediately and the monarch herself left Granton by sea on 15th September 1842. Exactly two years later the Duke of Buccleuch, in partnership with Sir John Gladstone, began his own ferry service to Burntisland using a sailing vessel and during 1846 this was replaced by a new steamer named FORTH which proved so successful that it soon saw off the long established Newhaven - Kinghorn and Leith - Kirkcaldy routes. Granton changed the fortunes of the hapless line from Scotland Street; in 1844 Parliament sanctioned a change of name to Edinburgh, Leith & Granton Railway, together with new branches from Trinity to Granton and Warriston to Leith and before long the financial press was describing the line as a valuable link in the grand chain of communications from England to the north of Scotland.

The mile long Granton extension veered west just before the original Trinity terminus and required rock excavations in the hillside behind Trinity Crescent before crossing Lower Granton Road on a stone bridge to reach the shoreline. It stayed close to high water mark before curving sharply north again on to the pier. The line opened on 19th February 1846 together with a very attractive new station at Trinity, leaving the old stub as a rather confined goods yard. Terminal facilities at Granton, in later years at least, consisted of a solitary wooden platform with a long but distinctly insalubrious timber building. Just over eleven weeks later, on 10th May 1846, the rails finally reached Leith. At Warriston the branch junction was squeezed in between the Water of Leith bridge and the first cutting on the Trinity route. The mile and a quarter line immediately turned north eastwards and crossed sloping ground leading down to the Water of Leith. At Bonnington it was virtually on the river bank for a couple of hundred yards, but soon entered a cutting below Newhaven Road where a station was provided. This cutting continued as far as Keddie Gardens where the now tidal Water of Leith provided company for a second time. A short tunnel under Junction Street and Coburg Street brought the branch to its terminus, facing Commercial Street.

Finally, the key section from Scotland Street to Canal Street (below Princes Street) opened on 17th May 1847 and it was in a wholly different league to the rest of the system. Almost all of the line was in a 1,052 yard tunnel which climbed at 1 in 27 towards the city centre and had a bore measuring 24ft wide by 17ft high. Excavations through folded and faulted strata made up of soft clay, hard sandstone and very tough whinstone were difficult enough for such a pioneering venture, but the New Town lay just above and six working shafts sunk between the elegant houses irritated many residents. From north to south the alignment followed Scotland Street itself, passed beneath Drummond Place, continued under Dublin Street and St. Andrew Street, and finally emerged below Princes Street. The tunnel was just a few feet below Scotland Street and had to contend with a tangle of drains and gas pipes, compared with a 35ft clearance beneath Princes Street and no less than 50ft of overlying rock midway along St. Andrew Street. It was gas lit and lined entirely with top quality masonry. Needless to say, on the opening day there were plenty of people eager to sample this novel transect of the New Town. Although the Edinburgh, Leith & Granton had replaced most if its horses with 0-4-0 locomotives, the gradient through the tunnel was far too steep for steam traction. Cable haulage was employed, a stationary winding engine at Canal Street controlling an endless rope six inches in circumference which ran under rollers between the rails, providing a steady ascent at about 10mph. Horses did at least find some employment, drawing carriages into the terminus. The descent was controlled by two hefty brake wagons marshalled at the front of each train, a tug from the winding engine starting the coaches rolling.

Canal Street station, actually called Princes Street for a while was a poor show. It had two impossibly short platforms and a network of goods sidings linked by a series of wagon turntables, all crammed into an area 100 yards square between Princes Street and Canal Street. The buildings were in a classical style, two storeys high, and access was by means of a steep ramp from Princes Street east of the tunnel mouth or a first floor entrance on Canal Street, which was carried on a viaduct at this point. The latter name harked back to an abortive scheme to extend the Union Canal from Fountainbridge to Leith. The Edinburgh & Glasgow station was at right angles on the opposite side of Canal Street and a tight westward facing spur connected the two systems. By mid-1847 there was a service of 25 trains each way between Edinburgh and Granton, with through coaches to Leith. Early morning departures, before the normal timetable commenced, provided connections with steamers to Kirkcaldy and Aberdeen. Two years later the pattern had been modified to give Leith a direct service at fifteen minute intervals and

Canal Street Station in 1847 - the south portal of Scotland Street tunnel can be seen on the lower left, with the train passing through what is now Princes Mall/Waverley Station

The Edinburgh, Leith & Granton station at North Leith was approached by a sharp curve and had the most restricted layout imaginable for what became an important suburban terminus. An apologetic overall roof provided a modicum of cover, but the modest North British locals, comprising a few old four-wheel coaches with a 4-4-0T in charge, were still largely out in the open even when right up against the buffer stops. An LNER Sentinel steam railcar, introduced in 1929, hardly managed to shelter beneath it either. Almost exactly ten years after passenger services finished, St. Margarets V3 2-6-2T No.67624 waited patiently at North Leith as fish vans were being loaded on 25th June 1957. The defiant grey stone bonded warehouse on the opposite side of Commercial Street still exists and continues to bear the legend 'Macdonald & Muir Highland Queen Whisky'. Photograph J.P. Wilson.

Granton a train every hour by means of through portions.

Well before achieving its final form, the Edinburgh, Leith & Granton was faced with takeover bids, notably from the Edinburgh & Glasgow which was building its extension through Princes Street Gardens from Haymarket to North Bridge. Tentative arrangements for amalgamation were made in 1845, but the union was never consummated. However on 27th July 1847 the local company was absorbed by the blossoming Edinburgh & Northern Railway which established a formidable network from Burntisland to Perth and Ferryport on Craig (later Tayport) in 1847-50, thus revolutionising transport between Edinburgh, Dundee and the north. Simultaneously the E&N managed to eliminate rival ferries at Granton and thus became the principal carrier across the Firth of Forth. The line from Canal Street really was part of a major trunk route now, despite its pedigree of bungling management and financial incompetence. The E&N was renamed Edinburgh, Perth & Dundee on 1st April 1849 and became a part of the North British empire on 29th July 1862.

By the mid-1860s the beginning of a journey from Edinburgh to Aberdeen in the confines of Scotland Street tunnel, sparks shooting from brake blocks to the accompaniment of an ear-piercing din, was decidedly unacceptable to most pas-

sengers. The brakesmen suffered even more and in harsh winters had to be helped down half frozen at Scotland Street. Furthermore, the tightly curved connection at Canal Street was becoming a real nuisance as it could only take four-wheel locos and carriages. Improved access to both Granton and Leith from Waverley station (as General, then North Bridge had become) was essential. The solution was a new two and a half mile route to Trinity from Piershill about 1¾ miles east of Waverley on the North British main line, thus bypassing most of the former Edinburgh, Leith & Granton alignment. From Piershill it ran north westwards and passed below Easter Road, Leith Walk, Broughton Road and Ferry Road before joining the earlier tracks at Trinity Junction just south of the tunnel. A sweeping curve from Easter Road to the main line at Abbeyhill allowed direct running from Waverley to the coast, and a short spur at Bonnington connected the new route to the North Leith branch which it crossed on the level. Goods traffic began on 2nd March 1868 and passenger services from Waverley to Leith and Granton followed on 22nd March 1868. New stations at Abbeyhill and Junction Road near North Leith opened on 1st May 1869. For further details of the new line see the Central Suburban chapter. As a result, passenger services through Scotland Street to Canal Street were with-

drawn on 22nd March 1868 and the latter station closed completely. The redundant tunnel then began a remarkable career involving a myriad of uses. For nearly twenty years it was used for storing wagons but in 1887 became a working railway again - albeit a highly unusual one. The dank and dark bore proved ideal for the purposes of the Scottish Mushroom Company which covered the down track with cultivation beds and used the up line for trucks bringing in fresh manure and removing exhausted beds. After many bountiful years supplying English markets, production had to cease in 1929 when a parasite infected the whole underground operation. Subsequent uses for the tunnel included a wartime bunker for LNER headquarters staff, safe from the *Luftwaffe*, a research laboratory for Edinburgh University, and storage space for a car dealer. The massive reconstruction of Waverley station in late Victorian times obliterated the site of Canal Street station and covered up the tunnel mouth, but the latter was rediscovered and finally destroyed during preparatory work for the new Waverley Centre in 1983. Nevertheless there is still a passageway leading to the deserted tunnel below the New Town, just a few yards from the escalators, fountains and glitter of the shopping mall.

After 1868 the rest of the Edinburgh, Leith & Granton system prospered under North British ownership and carried

Despite its inadequate interior, North Leith station presented an intriguing facade to Commercial Street. The single storey building, in grey stone, was slightly angled at the corner of Citadel Street, thus turning the entrance towards Leith town centre, albeit rather shyly. Classical details were employed, including round columns with highly decorative capitals flanking the main doorway, and more subdued square versions in the projecting section at the opposite end. There was a prominent cornice and the entrance was emphasised by little towers capped by urns. In 1914 North Leith had 26 weekday departures for Waverley, reduced to eleven by 1930 and down to six when it closed to passengers. The 'Steamboat Tavern', featuring a paddle vessel on its sign, occupied part of the building when this photograph was taken on 25th June 1957. Fortunately this historic terminus still survived in 1994, as an activities centre run by the Citadel Youth Project. Photograph J.P. Wilson.

its share of goods to and from the docks. Suburban passenger traffic developed as well, particularly on the North Leith branch. However, its traditional role as a route to the north was virtually terminated with the opening of the Forth Bridge in 1890 when Granton's four freight ferries were withdrawn and a solitary steamer was left to satisfy the residual passenger demand. Another blow came with the austerity measures required by World War I. On 1st January 1917 the ferry service was suspended together with local passenger trains from Edinburgh Waverley to Granton and North Leith. All were reinstated during 1919 but the economic situation had changed. Faced with mounting losses on so many of its peripheral operations, the LNER withdrew passenger trains from the Granton branch on 2nd November 1925 amid howls of protest. Although these were to no avail, specials occasionally ran. For example, on Saturday 27th May 1933 Wardie Church Sunday School ran an excursion for 80 adults and 200 youngsters from Granton to Ratho (with speed not to exceed 10mph from Granton to Bonnington North Junction) and on the same day a 300-strong Birkenhead Co-Operative Society party arrived at Burntisland (with speed reduced at Dalmeny so passengers could view the Forth Bridge) then crossed by ferry to

Granton where a special train was waiting to take them back to Waverley.

The ferry service from Granton was suspended by the LNER in March 1940 when the harbour became a base for minesweepers and complete abandonment was formally announced in December 1946. A new company started a vehicle ferry service in 1951 but this was doomed to failure; the opening of the Forth Road Bridge in 1964 effectively scuppered any further attempts. Meanwhile passenger trains to the cramped North Leith terminus ceased on 16th June 1947. With nearby facilities at Leith North and Leith Central soon to come under the same BR ownership, this seemed a logical rationalisation at the time. Over the next forty years goods traffic slipped away from the EL&G system as well; public facilities at Granton ceased to be available on 1st June 1960 whilst Junction Bridge depot, at the end of a short branch from Bonnington, closed on 1st August 1961. Scotland Street dealt with its last wagons of household coal on 6th November 1967 and the daily fish train from North Leith (actually Leith Citadel from May 1952) finished on 5th February 1968. Bonnington goods yard closed on 22nd July 1968. Finally, naptha traffic to Granton gasworks ceased on 20th January 1986 and the pioneering Edinburgh, Leith & Granton Railway was no more.

THE LOTHIAN LINES

East of Niddrie and south of Portobello a compact yet remarkable system of goods lines was woven round the existing and long established routes during 1915. Not only did this new network enhance the old Edinburgh & Dalkeith function of moving Lothian coal to Leith docks, but its immediate (and abortive) predecessor promulgated an astonishing motive power policy harking back to early 19th century practice.

Edwardian years saw a huge increase in output from the Lothian collieries and nearly three-quarters of the production was sent out by sea via South Leith. The line from Portobello to the quays had long been a bottleneck and became hopelessly congested as traffic grew during the early 1900s. Lothian coalowners were incensed by the delays but also regarded North British freight charges as excessive. In an attempt to break the main line company's monopoly and create a smoother passage for transhipments, they sought parliamentary approval for the Lothians Railway during 1912. This totally independent line, the last of its kind to be promoted in Central Scotland, was to run nearly thirteen miles from various pits south east of Edinburgh to Edinburgh Dock at Leith. A causeway, three quarters of a mile long, in the Firth of Forth, was planned from the outer limit of the

Bonnington station on Newhaven Road offered passenger facilities midway along the North Leith branch from the outset. It was a simple building with harsh walls of irregular grey sandstone, relieved by windows and doorways completely devoid of decoration. Moderately long platforms were provided, but tight clearances below the overbridge were dangerous for the unwary. At first the station building stood proud above the cutting, but four storey tenements on Newhaven Road soon dwarfed it. This photograph was taken on 15th October 1960, just after the track to North Leith had been singled. Today the former railway property is a couple of houses numbered 92 and 94 Newhaven Road, and still looks out of place amid its taller neighbours on the slope down to Water of Leith. The trackbed is now a walkway but the platforms remain.

new tracks were able to carry trains from 26th September 1915. No doubt construction work was hurried along as part of the war effort. Improvements were carried out to the dock approaches and the new line left the original Edinburgh & Dalkeith alignment as Seafield then ran parallel to it on a rising gradient as far as Portobello. A sweeping curve round the goods yard close to Portobello High Street followed, by which time the track was on a substantial embankment and still climbing. West of Joppa station it turned south and spanned the East Coast main line and Waverley route in quick succession. About quarter of a mile further on was Niddrie North Junction and here the Lothian lines began to descend on the existing layout in a masterly fashion. From a new high level Niddrie North Junction the mineral route divided into three separate tracks, one spur turning west to join the old St Leonards line at Niddrie West Junction, another continuing south to the Waverley route at Niddrie South Junction, and a third heading south eastwards for one and a quarter miles before meeting the East Coast main line at Monktonhall Junction. The whole of the Lothian coalfield had access to the system and for many years it was busy throughout the day and night, a situation which no doubt pleased local mineowners but was greeted with less enthusiasm by those living nearby. After a long period of decline, the Lothian lines closed on 9th January 1967 and Sir Harry Lauder Road has taken over its route from Portobello to Joppa forming a badly needed by pass for the main street in Portabello.

harbour to the shoreline at Seafield. This was unusual enough, but the expectation that individual operators would provide their own engines as well as wagons was quite extraordinary and would have revived a practice which more or less faded out with the end of horse traction. Naturally the North British opposed this scheme and the Bill failed in the House

of Lords after the company promised to upgrade traditional routes.

Authorisation for the North British Lothian lines came on 15th August 1913 after no problems in Parliament. The route mileage was considerably less than the original scheme and most of the system was single track, but engineering work was heavy and it is commendable that the

The Lothian Lines reflected the confidence brought about by over 80 years of railway construction in Edinburgh. Although the embankments carried just single track, they were hefty earthworks and the intervening underbridges consisted of solid-looking plate girders supported on brick abutments with red sandstone dressings. Signal boxes with hipped slate roofs stood tall and proud and, in keeping with the bridges, were functional rather than decorative in appearance. A smart-looking Gloucester diesel multiple unit forming the 12.49pm from Edinburgh Waverley to Gorgie East passed under the Lothian Lines at Niddrie North Junction on 16th July 1962. An impressive signal post controlling the parting of the ways for the three southern spurs can be seen beyond Niddrie North cabin.

Gresley A4 No.60004 WILLIAM WHITELAW sets out from Edinburgh Waverley on 25th July 1953, with the King's Cross-bound "Elizabethan" express. Photo: Brian Morrison

Chapter Two

Two Trunk Lines

Waverley Station and the lines west to Glasgow Queen Street and south to Berwick upon Tweed are the most widely known features of the Edinburgh railway network. The city's principal passenger station has long been one of the largest in the country and once boasted no less than 21 platforms. Yet it is also one of the least conspicuous and has always been barely noticeable from nearby Princes Street. The lines themselves were conceived as trunk routes, providing a link between Scotland's largest centres of population in the first instance, and part of a chain of railways down the east coast of Britain in the other. Both offered express services from the outset and have usually been worked ever since by the best rolling stock available, the latest examples being Class 158 diesel multiple units and InterCity 225 electrics respectively.

The Edinburgh & Glasgow Railway was Scotland's pioneering inter-city line and crossed the Forth - Clyde watershed by very gentle gradients, which required cuttings, embankments, viaducts and tunnels - on a scale massive for the time. It was an immediate success and has carried consistently heavy passenger traffic for over 150 years. Originally the Edinburgh terminus was at Haymarket, just west of the city centre, but an extension to North Bridge (later Waverley) was soon put in hand, thus providing an even more convenient gateway to Glasgow. A feeder line from Bathgate and Coatbridge brought some extra business, but 25 years after the Edinburgh & Glasgow lost its independence there was an enormous increase in trains through Haymarket, following the opening of the Forth Bridge. In marked contrast, local traffic immediately west of the city was sparse and none of the original stations between Linlithgow and Haymarket survived beyond 1951.

The North British Railway eventually became the largest company (railway or otherwise) in Scotland, yet its early years were characterised by faltering progress, dubious decisions and sheer bad luck. The original idea was sound enough - a line down the coast linking Edinburgh with Berwick upon Tweed ready to receive trains from London once the chain of rails through eastern England had been completed. This soon became a reality, but all too frequently the North British proved the weak link. Its northern terminus was at North Bridge and before long the station was also dealing with services from a number of straggling branch lines in remote Borders country. A remarkable network of suburban routes also developed to the east and south of Edinburgh, by

Class D34 No. 62490 GLEN FINTAIG arriving at Edinburgh Waverley on 25th July 1953, hauling a local service from North Berwick. Photo Brian Morrison.

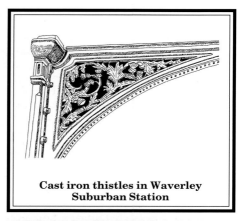

Cast iron thistles in Waverley Suburban Station

urday night. It lost money and was soon discontinued. Nevertheless the need for communication between the two cities was growing, and a twice weekly coach was introduced in 1749, and survived. By 1770 there were three coaches making the journey regularly, although it took up to twelve hours. Business grew substantially and in 1838 ten coaches carrying well over 300 passengers a day were on the road, the trip taking as little as four hours. Competition came from boat services using the Forth & Clyde and Union Canals; these had opened in 1790 and 1822 respectively and although the passage from

idea of laying tracks from Edinburgh to Glasgow never went away and an extension of the Garnkirk & Glasgow through Airdrie, Bathgate and Ratho was mooted during the early 1830s. The Edinburgh & Glasgow Railway itself was formed in 1835, and the promoters had a route surveyed through Falkirk, parallel to the Union and Forth & Clyde canals. Waterway opposition was implacable and the company had to struggle through three sessions of parliament before obtaining its Act, on 4th July 1838. The enormous task of building the line took less than three years despite unusually wet sum-

This nocturnal view of the east end of Waverley in pre-Grouping times was taken from the short footbridge connecting Leith Street with the Up Main through platform and No.8 bay. The long public footbridge across the station was beyond the third column and a siding veered off to the GPO loading bank on the extreme left. Clearly litter on the tracks is not a recent phenomenon! Photograph NRM.

which time the combined Edinburgh & Glasgow and North British stations at North Bridge had long been rechristened Waverley. The original route to Berwick upon Tweed is now a superb stretch of electrified main line and there is still a reasonable suburban service to North Berwick, but the rest of the system this side of the capital has passed into oblivion.

EDINBURGH & GLASGOW

The first attempt to provide public passenger services between Edinburgh and Glasgow was made in 1678 when a robust coach pulled by six horses left the capital on Monday morning and returned (God willing it was emphasised) on Sat-

Port Dundas in Glasgow to Port Hopetoun in Edinburgh took between seven and a half and eleven hours it was a less expensive option, and some 550 customers a day were taking advantage of it by 1838.

By the early 1820s there were numerous horse-operated waggonways in Great Britain and steam locomotives were beginning to prove themselves in the coalfields of north east England. When the public railway (as opposed to private lines built by individual canals or collieries) the steam engine and advertised passenger services came together with the Stockton & Darlington in 1825, there was an early dose of railway mania. Inevitably such bloated schemes as the Edinburgh, Leith, Glasgow, Paisley, Ardrossan & Troon Railway came to nought. However, the

mers, the inevitable awkwardness of some landowners, and the sheer scale of many engineering works. Up to 7,000 labourers employed by 21 contractors tackled the job, but most of the £1,200,000 required to finance it came from England. Passenger services between Edinburgh Haymarket and Glasgow Queen Street began on 21st February 1842, preceded forty eight hours earlier by a day of festivities for dignitaries and other invited guests. Goods traffic commenced in March 1842.

Unlike Queen Street station which enjoyed a convenient site in the centre of Glasgow, the Edinburgh terminus was on the western edge of the city. It was placed in a broad amphitheatre with ground rising northwards to the ridge on which the

The booking hall at Waverley had changed little since the early 1900s when this photograph was taken during the 1950s. With its dark cabinetwork, heavy stone mouldings and sombre Baroque theme, the place would have been overbearingly oppressive were it not for the glazed ceiling and splendid dome.

In common with other rooms off Waverley's main hall, the Seat Reservations Office had, to modern eyes, a pompous and frankly rather uninviting facade. Photographs W.E.A. Smith Collection.

New Town was built, eastwards to Castle Rock and southwards to Merchiston. Beyond Haymarket the track ran roughly south west, bisecting the angle between Corstorphine Road and Gorgie Road. The first mile descended at a gentle 1 in 1,250 with Dalry to the south and Roseburn to the north. At Murrayfield a bridge was required over the Water of Leith, by which time the gradient had changed to an ascent of 1 in 960, continuing thus for 11¾ miles. Corstorphine station, a couple of miles from Haymarket, was about threequarters of a mile away from the village, and here the Edinburgh & Glasgow occupied a low ridge between The Stank and Murray Burn, both tributaries of the Water of Leith. Corstorphine Hill was prominent to the north, whilst Craiglockhart Castle on its lofty perch and the distant Pentland Hills formed the southern skyline. At Sighthill the rails

ran on an embankment and veered west towards a bridge over the Gogar Burn. Nearby Gogar station, a little more than four miles out of the terminus and a mile from the tiny hamlet on Glasgow Road, was opened shortly after the line itself.

A series of sweeping curves followed, firstly north westwards through a cutting at Roddinglaw, and then west to Ratho, in order to avoid high ground formed by an outcrop of volcanic rocks. Ratho station, seven miles from Haymarket, was a mile and a quarter from the village, nestling below the southern slopes of the hill. Again the track swung north westwards and an embankment led to a massive 36 arch masonry viaduct over the River Almond and its water meadows. The embankment continued, punctuated a quarter mile further on by a smaller viaduct over the Beugh Burn. At Broomhouse, where the Union Canal briefly came

alongside, the engineers had to resort to a cutting. This led to the 372 yard Winchburgh tunnel through the neck of a long-extinct volcano. Winchburgh station, eleven miles from Edinburgh and close to the village for once, stood just north of the tunnel. Another steady curve brought the route back to a westerly alignment, the cutting continuing almost without a break for two and a half miles to Philpstoun, where a 1 in 887 descent began. At last the Edinburgh & Glasgow served an intermediate place of some importance; Linlithgow, just over sixteen miles from Haymarket, was an ancient town with a fine palace overlooking a natural lake. Ahead lay Falkirk, Croy, the Monklands plateau and Glasgow.

Passenger services began cautiously with four trains each way, starting at 7am, 11am, 3pm and 5pm from each terminus. Three of them stopped at all ten intermediate stations, taking two hours thirty minutes for the 46 mile journey, whilst the fastest timing was fifteen minutes less. Even this modest provision proved a shattering blow to the stagecoaches and the comprehensive operation which had blossomed over the previous nine decades collapsed within a month, apart from an early morning mail run. The Edinburgh & Glasgow was a huge success; soon there was a doubling of the service and improved timings of an hour and a half. Company forecasts, regarded by some observers as rather optimistic, put the number of passengers at nearly a thousand a day; in reality its trains carried an average of 1,600 people every day during the first ten months. Completely new opportunities for seeing the countryside arose, such as excursions to the Firth of Clyde and Ayrshire coast. This enthusiasm for travel mushroomed despite the standard of comfort on offer, for although first class passengers enjoyed stagecoachlike vehicles with windows and plush upholstery, those travelling second class had to endure draughty carriages with open sides, whilst the poor souls with third class tickets mainly stood in open wagons. Traffic control was equally primitive, for there was very little signalling and trains followed the previous departure after a prescribed time interval had elapsed.

It soon became apparent that a more convenient terminus in the centre of Edinburgh was essential and an extension from Haymarket to North Bridge, adjacent to the proposed North British facilities, was planned. The new mileage was sanctioned on 4th July 1844, at the same time as the line from Berwick upon Tweed. Thus far, the Forth & Clyde and Union Canals had managed to maintain a passenger service between Edinburgh and Glasgow, but rightly regarded these fresh railway developments as a very serious threat. Rather than surrender, the boat operators retaliated with even faster

The youthful days of Edinburgh's principal station are beautifully portrayed in this view of Waverley Bridge from Princes Street Gardens, probably in 1865. On the left is the North British entrance building, a simple classical structure with a prominent arcade. Alongside, a large hoarding proclaims **North British & Scottish Central Railways to Perth, Aberdeen, Inverness and The North via Larbert & Stirling without change of carriage.** *The approach tracks are congested with four and six wheel coaches, those nearest the camera standing on the curve to Canal Street station. St. Giles cathedral is a distinctive feature of the Old Town skyline to the right, but note also the nine storey tenements towering above Cockburn Street. Photograph BCJT.*

2-2s, and finally a series of 2-4-0s which were working principal trains when the company was absorbed by the North British Railway on 1st August 1865. The ubiquitous 4-4-0 type made its debut on Edinburgh - Glasgow expresses during 1871. Meanwhile the line from Ratho to South Queensferry had brought a few more customers since 1868, but the much shorter Caledonian route to Glasgow (via Shotts) proved highly competitive from 1869 and forced Waverley - Queen Street timings down to an hour and twenty minutes. An alternative North British link with Glasgow, via Bathgate, Coatbridge and Airdrie, was completed in December 1870 although it was not a railway conducive to speed. Philipstoun station, between Winchburgh and Linlithgow, opened on 12th October 1885 whilst the Forth Bridge and its approach lines from Saughton Junction and Winchburgh Junction were completed during 1890, adding an enormous number of trains to Edinburgh's western approach lines. In fact congestion soon became chronic and the North British was deluged with complaints about delays to passenger and goods trains alike. The only solution was to quadruple the line through Haymarket and Princes Street Gardens but inevitably there was a deafening chorus of protest. However, there was no alternative and the widening was sanctioned on 5th July 1891, the new tracks and tunnels being completed during the summer of 1895. Corstorphine station was renamed Saughton on 1st February 1902 when a short branch to the village centre opened.

Holmes 4-4-0s, including some with 7ft

timings and a poster issued in the autumn of 1845 showed a barge skimming along behind galloping horses being whipped by the rider. Inevitably, as the new lines took shape, this proved a rather ridiculous swansong. The Edinburgh & Glasgow incurred the wrath of many citizens as it had to carve a path through Princes Street Gardens immediately below the Castle Rock. Fortunately this section was in a cutting and therefore fairly unobtrusive. From Haymarket the line dropped at 1 in 500 through Haymarket tunnel (1,009 yards) before levelling out past the gardens. A rise of 1 in 500 took it through The Mound tunnel (124 yards) and on to Canal Street where there was an end-on connection with the North British at what was effectively a through station. This mile and a quarter of double track opened on 1st August 1846, a few weeks after the line from the south.

By the end of 1847 the Edinburgh & Glasgow was carrying some 3,000 passengers a day and waterway competition had ceased. In fact the Union Canal was purchased by the railway in 1849, subsequently settling down as a major conveyor of minerals. Increased traffic came with the opening of the Bathgate branch from Ratho on 12th November 1849, but a new rival had emerged in the form of the Caledonian route from Edinburgh to Glasgow via Carstairs. A frantic and potentially ruinous price war ensued until sense prevailed early in 1850. By then the

Edinburgh & Glasgow was a substantial business operating 58 locomotives, 216 carriages and 374 wagons. Motive power consisted of Bury and Hawthorn single wheelers at first, then Beyer Peacock 2-

Today, this viewpoint on North Bridge would reveal acres of glass roof covering the east end of Waverley, but in 1865 it showed a hotchpotch of track and goods facilities marking the original North British approach to Edinburgh. The detail is fascinating. In marked contrast to the deep stone bed familiar nowadays, ash ballast up to rail level served for the main running lines, in the right foreground. The general goods yard on the left contained stacks of pipes, possible for water or sewerage schemes, and several open wagons had sheeting revealing their ownership - including 'NER' and 'S. CENTRAL'. Photograph BAJT.

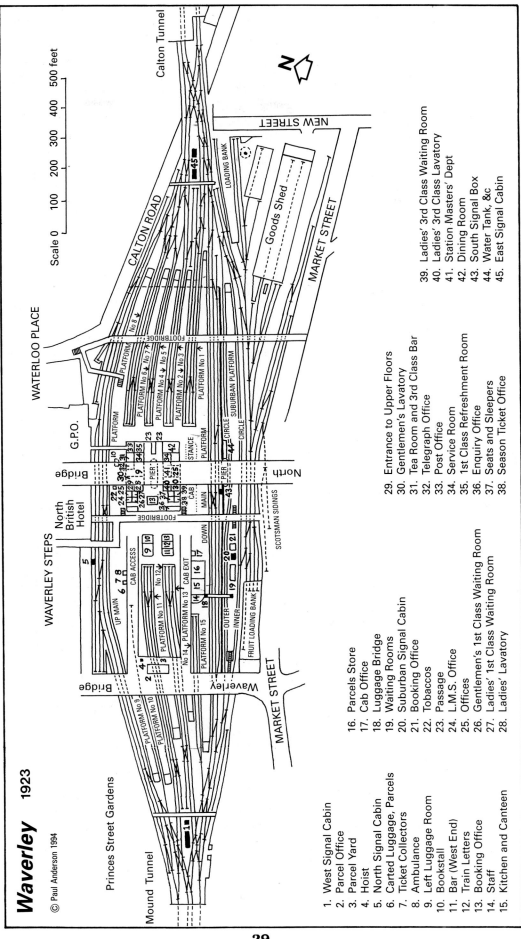

Waverley 1923

© Paul Anderson 1994

Scale 0   100 200 300 400 500 feet

1. West Signal Cabin
2. Parcel Office
3. Parcel Yard
4. Hoist
5. North Signal Cabin
6. Carted Luggage, Parcels
7. Ticket Collectors
8. Ambulance
9. Left Luggage Room
10. Bookstall
11. Bar (West End)
12. Train Letters
13. Booking Office
14. Staff
15. Kitchen and Canteen

16. Parcels Store
17. Cab Office
18. Luggage Bridge
19. Waiting Rooms
20. Suburban Signal Cabin
21. Booking Office
22. Tobaccos
23. Passage
24. L.M.S. Office
25. Offices
26. Gentlemen's 1st Class Waiting Room
27. Ladies' 1st Class Waiting Room
28. Ladies' Lavatory

29. Entrance to Upper Floors
30. Gentlemen's Lavatory
31. Tea Room and 3rd Class Bar
32. Telegraph Office
33. Post Office
34. Service Room
35. 1st Class Refreshment Room
36. Enquiry Office
37. Seats and Sleepers
38. Season Ticket Office

39. Ladies' 3rd Class Waiting Room
40. Ladies' 3rd Class Lavatory
41. Station Masters' Dept
42. Dining Room
43. South Signal Box
44. Water Tank, &c
45. East Signal Cabin

In this period piece at Waverley around 1929, the crew of K3 2-6-0 No.32 posed for the photographer. The backdrop of buildings in Jeffrey Street remains today but the goods station off to the left is now a car park and the public footbridge across the eastern platforms has also gone. The locomotive, shedded at Carlisle Canal, had been built at Darlington in 1924 and was fitted with a Great Northern style tender. Renumbered 1812 in 1946, it was scrapped as BR 61812 in 1962. Photograph J.J. Cunningham.

The rebuilt North Bridge of 1897 was not only a bold, confident, structure but a fairly decorative one as well. Along with the new Waverley the styling was classical, as demonstrated by the little pediments incorporated in the parapet and garlands festooning both the stone piers and metal spans. With the GPO and Register House in the background and a rather untidy part of Waverley station below, tram No.196 on service 17 to Newington station crossed North Bridge on 19th November 1955.

driving wheels, had been used for expresses since their introduction during the 1880s and regular 65 minute timings were possible by the turn of the century. 'Scott' 4-4-0s (LNER classes D29 and D30) arrived in 1909/12 and the 'Lothian Coast Express' (making its first run during 1912) was the first regular daily service between the two cities in an even hour. Dilatory all stations trains at this time were taking a monumental *two hours* - hardly an improvement on the 1840s! The 'Scotts' reigned until the Scottish 'Directors' (class D11/2) were built in 1924 but these in turn were partly superseded by the 'Shires' (class D49/1) in 1927 and even more so by Gresley Pacifics from the mid-1930s. North Eastern Railway Atlantics employed on the East Coast Main Line also ventured on to the Edinburgh & Glasgow at this time and in 1939 the massive P2 2-8-2s, based at Haymarket for the Aberdeen road, had a couple of turns on the route.

By 1938 the best timing (by a mid afternoon train) was down to 58 minutes. Despite the inevitable austerity measures, maintained during World War II, a somewhat astonishing 65 minute schedule was regularly achieved by a 4-4-0 hauling ten or more coaches on the 4.00pm departure from Waverley. Ex-Great Eastern Railway class B12 4-6-0s, far away from East Anglia but perhaps at home on the easy gradients, were tried during the war. By 1948 the service had reverted to hourly with a best time of sixty minutes and Gresley, Thompson and Peppercorn Pacifics, together with V2 2-6-2s and new B1 4-6-0s, monopolised the route. A D11 occasionally appeared and oddities such as the Gresley V4s (61700/1) and ex-LMS Ivatt moguls could also be seen.

From 1842 to 1957 motive power for Scotland's principal inter-city route was provided by Haymarket shed. Originally this consisted of a small building just a few hundred yards out of Haymarket station, but it was rebuilt further west - still on the north side of the main line - with the track quadrupling in 1894. The new layout was generous and included an eight road shed, later to be dominated by the huge concrete mechanical coaling plant installed by the LNER. In pre-grouping years it provided engines principally for

services to the north and west of Edinburgh, but after 1923 became almost exclusively an express passenger depot, with an enviable reputation for well turned out locomotives.

Although the Edinburgh & Glasgow has been one of the great success stories in the history of Britain's railways, there were one or two casualties along the way. Saughton station was ill-suited to local passenger needs once the Corstorphine branch opened and it finally expired on 1st March 1921 after a wartime shutdown from 1st January 1917 to 1st February 1919. The remoteness of many intermediate stopping places became painfully apparent once local bus services were established and trains ceased to call at Gogar and Winchburgh on 22nd September 1930, with Ratho and Philipstoun following them into oblivion on 18th June 1951. Gogar lost its goods facilities on 1st March 1960 and the yards at Saughton and Philipstoun closed on 24th February and 23rd March 1964 respectively. Swindon-built inter-city diesel multiple units, complete with buffets, were introduced in January 1957 and covered the 47 1/4 miles between Waverley and Queen Street in 55 minutes. Push-pull Mk2 sets with a Birmingham RCW diesel (class 27) at either end took over in May 1971 and reduced the journey time to 43 minutes. Class 47s with Mk3 coaches and a Mk2 driving trailer replaced them in December 1980 and managed 42 minutes with one stop at Haymarket. Since 1990 class 158 diesel units have provided a half-hourly service making the journey in as little as fifty minutes with just three stops.

The marshalling of passenger and parcels vehicles was an essential feature of operations at Waverley until fairly recently. On 18th May 1957 west end pilot J83 0-6-0T No.68474 stood at rest during a spell of duty. This had been one of the engines painted apple green under the LNER's imaginative post-war scheme, but by the time the photograph was taken it was in the dignified BR lined black passenger livery. Early in 1959 the four Waverley pilots were replaced by diesel shunters. Photo: Brian Morrison.

This grand panorama from the site of Calton Jail admirably demonstrates the relationship between Waverley and the Old Town. The graceful arches of North Bridge stride across the valley up to the great pile of buildings rising from Edinburgh's Royal Mile, whilst a touch of mist softens Castle Rock in the distance. Calton Road dives under the eastern approach tracks in the foreground and goods facilities occupy much of the middle left. East end bay platforms, once serving most places in the arc between Granton and Gorgie, peep from beneath the overall roof. It was 7th March 1959 and Gresley A3 Pacific No.60082 NEIL GOW added a touch of life to the grey day as it departed with the 12.05pm up 'Queen of Scots' Pullman for London King's Cross, having taken over from A4 No.60024 KINGFISHER which had brought the train in from Glasgow Queen Street.

NORTH BRITISH

By the dawn of 1842 a growing network of railways was beginning to link the major cities of England, whilst in Scotland the Edinburgh & Glasgow was almost ready and the west coast towns of Greenock and Ayr already had trains from Glasgow. The stage was set for a line across the border and much excitement surrounded such schemes over the next few years. However, the mighty east coast route started in a hesitant way, despite its promise. Just over six weeks before the Edinburgh & Glasgow opened, the company hosted a meeting at its headquarters where a railway from the capital to Berwick upon Tweed was discussed. The promoters clearly got cold feet about such a large project and decided to proceed cautiously with a modest line to Dunbar, through the wheat fields of Haddingtonshire. Local worthies were unimpressed and looked elsewhere to reap profits from their share subscriptions. This prompted a re-think and the embryo North British company decided that the huge triangle of Border country between Edinburgh, Carlisle and Berwick upon Tweed was ripe for railway development and pressed ahead with its complete east coast project. This time finance was readily forthcoming, but largely from south of the border. Stagecoach services operated along the Great North Road and there were popular sailings between Leith and London but both took a long time and the English investors were convinced that

a railway would be guaranteed success. In marked contrast to the Edinburgh & Glasgow's experience, the North British sailed through Parliament and gained its Act on 4th July 1844 with little opposition. Even recalcitrant landowners were quickly pacified. Construction began almost immediately on the main line and a branch, four and a half miles long, from Longniddry to Haddington. This historic and important Lothian town was eager to secure a place on what promised to be an Anglo-Scottish trunk route, but was by-passed because of the extra expendi-

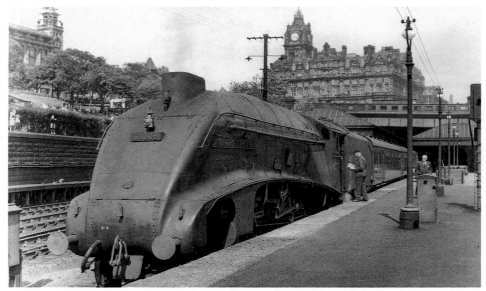

In brilliant afternoon sunshine on 20th July 1959, plenty of people sat in Princes Street Gardens absorbing the warmth or cooling down in the shade of trees. However, a few youngsters clinging to the railings had found something more interesting to do. They were clearly fascinated by Haymarket A4 Pacific No.60009 UNION OF SOUTH AFRICA, simmering at Waverley's platform 16 in charge of the 4.00pm to Perth via Glenfarg. The train included through carriages for Inverness. The elegant bulk of the North British Hotel dominated Waverley Bridge, where Edinburgh Corporation coaches waited to leave with sightseeing tours of the city.

There was plenty of sunshine on 7th November 1959, but nobody tarried in the gardens and the trees were decidedly bare as B1 4-6-0 No.61403 made a lively start from Waverley with the 12.15pm to Cardenden. The train of mixed LNER and LMS non-corridor stock served Dunfermline Lower after crossing the Forth Bridge. Although the Thornton engine was looking remarkably smart, it seemed determined to send a dense cloud of clag in the direction of the North British Hotel!

V3 2-6-2T No.67615 was rostered for the 12.35pm local from Waverley to Corstorphine on 7th November 1959, the train consisting of Thompson and BR standard main line corridor stock. In the background a Swindon Intercity diesel multiple unit bound for Glasgow Queen Street waited for departure time.

ture required. Like the Edinburgh & Glasgow, the North British was built quickly - in less than two years as it turned out. But the similarity stopped there. Earthworks were kept to a minimum and the line see-sawed over relatively gentle contours as far as Dunbar with no attempt to match the bold course of the line to Glasgow. Hard-pressed contractors produced some extremely dubious work and several bridges and embankments showed structural weaknesses well before the railway opened. Although the North British had been built hurriedly, in piecemeal fashion, any doubts as to its ability to cope in the future were cast aside on 18th June 1846, when a grand extravaganza celebrated its completion. Two trains of sparkling maroon coaches hauled by new 0-4-2 locos conveyed guests from Edinburgh to Berwick upon Tweed and back to North Bridge. Public services be-

gan on 22nd June 1846 and the first line between Scotland and England was in business.

From North Bridge the line had to drop from the narrow rift between Calton Hill and Holyrood to the coastal plain, the resultant mile long gradient of 1 in 78 through Abbeyhill being the steepest on the line (and eventually the most severe on the whole Waverley - Kings Cross route). To complicate matters, a 398 yard tunnel through the southern flank of Calton Hill was also necessary. At Meadowbank the descent eased to 1 in 300 and at this point St. Margarets shed and works were established close to the skew bridge carrying London Road across the rails. A station called Jock's Lodge was provided just to the east near Restalrig Road (a mile and a half from North Bridge) but it closed on 1st July 1848 when a single platform on the Edin-

burgh - bound track opened west of London Road (a mile and a quarter from North Bridge). Although officially called Meadowbank, it was also known as Queens, through its proximity to Holyrood House and occasional royal patronage. After another skew bridge under Portobello Road, the line headed south east to Portobello itself where a level stretch crossed Friggate Burn on a two arch bridge and the Edinburgh & Dalkeith's South Leith branch on an eleven span timber and iron viaduct in quick succession. Portobello station, two and three quarters of a mile from the Edinburgh terminus, was immediately beyond these bridges. In response to the minor undulations of the coastal plain, the North British climbed at 1 in 400 past Joppa, breasted a low summit at Newhailes and descended at 1 in 300 to a twin span bridge over the River Esk. Joppa station 3 1/2 miles from North Bridge, was on Brunstane Road and opened on 16th July 1847, when the Musselburgh branch service began. The original Musselburgh station (six miles and a half from Edinburgh and a mile from the town centre) stood half a mile east of Esk bridge on the main line. It was renamed Inveresk when the town gained its new terminus.

Beyond Inveresk there was a gentle three mile ascent, mainly at 1 in 300, where the escarpment forming Falside Hill approached the coast. There was a short cutting, followed by an embankment near the site of the Battle of Pinkie and a longer cutting at Wallyford, bridged by the Great North Road. Tranent station (renamed Prestonpans for Tranent on 1st July 1858) was 9 1/2 miles from North Bridge and stood roughly midway between the two settlements which appeared on its nameboards. After crossing the even more famous battlefield of Prestonpans, the North British rose and fell with the contours as it crossed minor streams draining to the Firth of Forth. Cockenzie, a mile away on the coast, was clearly deemed too close to Prestonpans to warrant separate facilities. Longniddry station (a little under thirteen miles from Edinburgh) was important from the outset as it served as the junction for the Haddington branch, which opened with the main line. Another climb at 1 in 300 took the tracks to Spittal and a short descent on an embankment led to a level stretch through Ballencrieff, sixteen miles from North Bridge. Although this station had a coach connection to Aberlady and Gullane on the coast, receipts were abysmal and it closed on 1st November 1847. A two mile drop at 1 in 300 took the North British to its lowest point so far and midway along this section was Drem, nearly eighteen miles from Edinburgh and soon to be the junction for the North Berwick branch. Ahead lay Dunbar, the long slog up to Grantshouse, and the Tweed estuary.

Regular services on the North British Railway began with five trains each way between Edinburgh and Berwick, where there were stagecoach connections to and from Newcastle. The best timing, with just one intermediate stop at Dunbar, was an hour and a half, in marked contrast to the all stations workings which took two and a half. In addition some ten locals ran to Musselburgh, giving the town a remarkable service for those early days - for most through trains called as well. Rolling stock was of a higher standard than that on most contemporary lines; first class vehicles followed the stagecoach pattern as expected, but second class travellers also had enclosed carriages with windows, providing a fair amount of comfort despite their box-like appearance. Even third class passengers were treated to roofs and benches. Motive power con-

sisted of 26 double-framed 0-4-2s manufactured by Hawthorn of Newcastle, followed by six 2-2-2s and fifteen 2-4-0s from the same builder. Successive batches of 0-6-0s hauled both the established Lothian coal flows and developing agricultural traffic from the Borders.

Despite its promising start, the young North British was soon dealt a heavy blow -largely resulting from economic restraints during its construction. September 1846 was very wet and the fragile trackbed fell apart in several places as floodwater washed away bridges and embankments along the coast. Repairs were executed with alacrity, but when the trains began running again the main concern was a paucity of customers. Although stagecoach services along the parallel Great North Road had surrendered almost immediately, steamers from Leith

to London were carrying twice as many through passengers as the trains. North British fortunes nevertheless soon began to change, thanks to developments beyond its territory. The Newcastle & Berwick Railway opened its line to Tweedmouth on 1st July 1847 and the magnificent Royal Border Bridge across the Tweed carried regular services from 29th August 1850. Journey times to London were halved and when the Great Exhibition was staged during 1851, Edinburgh's citizens surged south by rail. Meanwhile local goods traffic was flourishing too, with a 4.30am departure from Berwick bringing farm produce to Waverley Market next to North Bridge station and daily herring trains running from Dunbar.

Given that it experienced an uneasy succession of Locomotive Superintendents, it is hardly surprising that the North

Even as recently as the early 1960s the glory and glamour of the steam age was not quite over and Edinburgh was one of the places where it could still be witnessed. On 15th August 1961 Gresley A4 Pacific No.60030 GOLDEN FLEECE rolled into Platform 10/11 at Waverley with the non-stop 'Elizabethan' express, at the end of its 393 mile journey from London. The train had left King's Cross at 9.30am and arrived in the Scottish capital at 4.13pm, an acceptable eight minutes late. By a fortuitous coincidence, sunlight illuminated the engine and made it the star of the show, as then-modern Standard Vanguard and Ford Consul cars picked up passengers.

On 2nd September 1952 Haymarket Pacific No.60096 PAPYRUS pulled out of Waverley with the 2.00pm up 'Heart of Midlothian' express for London King's Cross. The fireman took a brief rest, having prepared his engine to perfection - the exhaust was clean and just a wisp of steam escaped from the safety valves. St. Andrew's House, the Scottish Office building erected on the site of Calton Jail in 1937, rears above the tracks. Some ramparts from the old prison survive on the right and the governor's house, a rather whimsical creation, towered above the platforms off to the left. Calton tunnel with its unusual stepped portal was just out of sight to the right. The 'Heart of Midlothian' was named for the 1951 Festival of Britain.

British found difficulty coping with this popularity and there is some evidence that engines had to be hired from the North Eastern Railway (which had inherited the Newcastle - Berwick route) during the late 1850s. In 1862 the English company obtained running powers between Berwick and Edinburgh, although these were not exercised until 1869 when it took over the through East Coast Joint Stock trains, using Fletcher and later Tennant 2-4-0s. The North British was left with four local workings each way. After the famous Railway Races to Edinburgh in 1888 and Aberdeen during 1895, the Scottish board attempted to evict its neighbour. One outcome of this was a considerable amount of double heading by Drummond and Holmes 4-4-0s on expresses from 1897 but the North Eastern was soon back again using sturdy Worsdell 4-4-0s, then the graceful Raven Atlantics. Meanwhile rolling stock on the main line had improved dramatically since the early four wheel coaches, and most Edwardian East Coast expresses consisted of luxurious corridor bogie vehicles, including dining cars. With the London & North Eastern Railway came the Gresley Pacifics and these magnificent machines assisted by later Thompson and Peppercorn variants and V2 2-6-2s were to reign supreme through nationalisation until the advent of diesel traction.

Away from the Edinburgh area, local services over the North British main line have always been fairly sparse. In 1913 there were only three stopping trains between Edinburgh and Berwick, taking up to two hours twenty minutes, although a fourth journey was possible by a change

of trains and a 41 minute wait at Dunbar. By 1930 there were four trains calling at fifteen intermediate stations, taking

about two hours but supplemented by several expresses pausing at Berwick an hour and fifteen minutes after leaving Edinburgh. Nationalisation brought little change, but by 1962 the local service was down to two workings each way taking hour and three quarters and the number of through trains calling at Berwick had risen to about a dozen each way. In steam days motive power for most of the slow trains was supplied by St. Margarets shed on the eastern approach to Waverley. This depot existed on the same site for over 120 years and had its days of glory before Haymarket took over the most prestigious workings. In 1846 a semi-roundhouse was erected on the north side of the tracks and construction of a workshop began as well. The latter eventually built locomotives besides repairing them until eclipsed by Glasgow's Cowlairs Works, inherited from the Edinburgh & Glasgow Railway. St. Margarets gained a six-road shed south of the main line during the mid-1860s and facilities for North Eastern engines appeared about the same time. Locos from south of the border continued to be stabled here until about 1904 when they were transferred to Haymarket. A large proportion of the St. Margarets locomotive shed allocation - there was something over 200 engines at the depot for many years - was employed on Lothians

In this panoramic view of the west end of Waverley station on 29th August 1964, Fairburn 2-6-4T No.42128 departed from platform 11 with the 11.40am to Stirling as a Swindon Intercity set waited at platform 12 with the 12 noon departure for Glasgow Queen Street. The scene is deceptively quiet, for closer inspection reveals diesel multiple units hiding beneath the canopies at platforms 15 and 17, with local services for Fife. As ever, the North British Hotel dominated the scene, but just to the right of it the extraordinary collection of architecture festooning Calton Hill also got a look in, including the unfinished National Monument based on the Parthenon, the Nelson Monument shaped like an upturned telescope, and the castellated Governor's House of Calton Jail. Waverley's main parcels office (on the site of the original station entrance and now a restaurant) is just visible on the bridge, and the suburban island platform can be seen to the right, separated from the main part of the station by a granite wall.

Seen in the guise of The Balmoral, the former North British Hotel looked particularly impressive against billowing clouds in low evening sunshine on 9th June 1994. The immensely complex and extravagant building rose to five storeys and each one had its own architectural characteristics. Ionic columns and large round-headed windows were features of the ground and first floors, the latter also having balconies. The second storey had smaller windows, with alternating triangular and segmental hoods, whilst the third floor had big brackets supporting a pronounced cornice with dentilled (that is, tooth-like) mouldings. Finally a riot of flamboyant gables, projecting turrets, flattened domes, little dormers and tall chimneys formed a combined fifth storey and roof line. Crowns were a recurring motif, over twenty of them capping the turrets and a particularly ornate one providing a finishing touch to the mighty tower 183ft above the pavement. Photograph Paul Anderson.

Arriving at Edinburgh Waverley on 25th July 1953, Gresley V1 class 2-6-2T No. 67659 powers the 8.16am local train from North Berwick. Photograph Brian Morrison.

coal traffic and dock work but suburban passenger trains and Waverley route expresses also featured in rosters. Because of the cramped nature of the site, sub-sheds and other stabling points were essential to its operation.

Apart from early closures such as Ballencrieff in 1847, and Jock's Lodge in 1848, there were few major developments pertaining to local stations on the North British trunk in the Edinburgh area for well over a century. Tranent was renamed Prestonpans on 1st July 1858 and Inveresk acquired the suffix 'Junction' between 1st October 1876 and 2nd June 1890. Joppa station was relocated on the main line in 1859 (having previously been situated on the Hawick branch) whilst Portobello was rebuilt with a generous island platform during 1887. Seton Mains

Halt, between Prestonpans and Longniddry, opened on 1st May 1914 to serve Seton Sands, or possibly more distant Port Seton, and lasted until 22nd September 1930. Goods facilities were withdrawn from remote Ballencrieff on 1st January 1959 some 111 years after the passenger trains, and others were picked off one at a time during the 1960s - for example, Longniddry on 28th December 1964, Inveresk on 25th January 1965, Edinburgh Waverley on 2nd January 1967 and Prestonpans on 5th February 1968. Passenger trains stopped calling at Inveresk on 4th May 1964, followed by the closure of Portobello and Joppa on 7th September 1964 when the Musselburgh service was withdrawn. Prestonpans, Longniddry and Drem remained open as intermediate stops for North Berwick locals although they were threatened with closure in 1968.

English Electric Type 4s took over some East Coast expresses in 1958, but the real diesel revolution came with the fleet of Deltics which began to make an impact on overall timings from 1961. Several were stabled at Haymarket and they proved worthy successors to the Pacifics, although non-stop runs between Edinburgh and Berwick still took a minimum of 53 minutes in 1968. InterCity 125s began to take over Deltic turns in 1978 and over the next few years schedules to King's Cross were improved even more, with the Waverley - Berwick time down to 41 minutes by 1988. HSTs were provided with specially built maintenance facilities at Craigentinny and this heralded the end of Haymarket (St. Margarets had closed way back in 1966) as a main line depot. Electrification of the East Coast main line was announced in 1984 and further work was carried out at Craigentinny to accommodate class 91 electric locos and Mk 4 coaches. The full Anglo-Scottish service began on 8th July 1991 but there is little scope for the new trains to show their full potential on the North British section and in 1994 39 minutes was allowed for the fastest Edinburgh - Berwick run. Beeching cuts had wiped out the remaining main line stopping services thirty years previously but Prestonpans, Longniddry and Drem, together with new stations at Musselburgh and Wallyford, enjoyed an hourly service of electric suburban trains running to and from North Berwick.

WAVERLEY

Edinburgh Waverley is by far the most unusual of Britain's main line stations. It covers a vast area, yet many of the busiest parts are quite claustrophobic. Let alone a grand facade, there is nothing whatsoever to welcome passengers and access is by means of narrow pavements alongside the Waverley Bridge cab ramps or a grim stairway from Princes Street between towering stone walls. Neverthe-

Class 5 4-6-0 No.45396 sent a cloud of smoke up to the elegant portico and balustrades of the National Gallery of Scotland as it burst out of The Mound tunnel and into Princes Street Gardens with the 11.40am from Edinburgh Waverley to Stirling via Falkirk, on 17th November 1964. Although St. Margarets had some Stanier class 5s by this time, the loco was allocated to Stirling. Numerous footpaths crossed the gardens; the wall midway up the bank above the tunnel identifies one of them and the photograph was taken from another, where it spanned the tracks on a lattice bridge.

less, at rail level there is some remarkably fine classical detail in wood and metal, whilst the main amenity block is particularly opulent. The overall roof and platform canopies are also very impressive. Several factors determined the unique character of the station, notably its sunken location in the hollow between Castle Rock and the New Town, and a 40ft height restriction imposed by the city authorities. Huge traffic demands and the need to provide something befitting the capital of Scotland also influenced North British architects when they designed the new Waverley a century ago. Although it is basically a through station consisting of an enormous island platform, most expresses, medium distance services and suburban trains have always terminated here. No less than 15 bays cut into the ends of the island helped to satisfy these requirements.

Armed with a plan of the original layout and a certain amount of imagination, the early years of Waverley can just about be recreated during an amble round the present station. Princes Street to the north, Market Street on the southern flank and the spans of Waverley Bridge and North Bridge provide a grid which has remained more or less fixed over the last 150 years. Canal Street, which passed east - west through the middle of the site and influenced the original track layout, was totally obliterated many years ago however. North British and Edinburgh & Glasgow trains terminated at a two-platform through station immediately south of the erstwhile Canal Street, between Waverley Bridge and North Bridge; there were three lines separating the platform roads with rows of small turntables at either end and in the middle of the station, allowing carriages to be transferred between tracks. The Edinburgh & Glasgow booking office was on Waverley Bridge whilst the North British facilities were near North Bridge. Cramped goods stations stood next to Market Street and near Waterloo Place respectively. On the north side of Canal Street, the Edinburgh, Leith & Granton terminated at right angles to the main line and was connected to the Glasgow route by a north to west curve, as described in Chapter One. An overall roof made up of longitudinal gables in iron and glass covered the through station but it was a poor show. There was even uncertainty about the name and the station was variously referred to as Waverley Bridge, North Bridge, Canal Street, General or just plain Edinburgh right up to the 1860s, although Edinburgh Waverley was becoming an accepted title by this time.

When Granton and North Leith trains were diverted into the east end of Waverley during 1868, overcrowding became a serious problem. However, the demise of the Canal Street terminus did at least provide a partial solution. Waverley Market, originally situated on Market Street below North Bridge, was moved to the former station site and the land thus released was used to rearrange the layout and expand the platform area. Work proceeded in a piecemeal fashion between 1869 and 1873, eventually providing five passenger lines. A relentless increase in traffic soon cancelled out the improvements and services on new branches in the Edinburgh area also had to be accommodated. Matters came to a head with the opening of the Forth Bridge in 1891. Apart from acute difficulties associated with the sheer number of trains using Waverley, there was clutter and confusion on the narrow platforms and passengers were at risk. Waiting rooms

The glory of Edinburgh city centre is very apparent in this view from above The Mound tunnel as class 5 No.45183 drifted through Princes Street Gardens with the 10.15am from Stirling to Edinburgh Waverley on 26th September 1964. Princes Street itself is in the right background and the magnificent Caledonian Hotel stands proudly on the skyline. The spire in front of it belongs to St. Cuthbert's Kirk at the west end of the gardens, and the church with the tower is St. John's at the corner of Lothian Road. Castle rock and the little Queen's Post Tower is just visible on the left. It is quite remarkable how the four track main line managed to slip barely noticed through this lovely setting.

With few simultaneous departures from the west end of Waverley over the years, there was little scope for unofficial racing on the four track section from Waverley to Saughton Junction, but a notable exception occurred in mid-afternoon during the 1950s. On 29th August 1955 platelayers stood back as Gresley A3 No.60100 SPEARMINT and Peppercorn A2 No.60536 TRIMBUSH pounded through Princes Street Gardens with the 4.00pm expresses to Perth and Glasgow Queen Street respectively. The former consisted largely of ex-LNER Gresley coaches whilst the latter was composed of BR standard stock.

and other facilities were woefully inadequate and merchandise from the congested goods yards spilled over into public areas. The chaos had to be sorted out, so the North British acquired powers for a complete reconstruction on 5th July 1890, at the same time as the quadrupling from Saughton Junction was approved. This massive undertaking took from 1892 to 1900 and cost £1,500,000, but the overall result was magnificent. North Bridge, originally built in 1772 with eleven irregular arches, and an irritating obstacle to the railway, was reconstructed and incorporated in the station during 1897.

In its final form Waverley occupied 23 acres of which precisely half was under glass. The up main platform on the north side curved at either end and was 1,607ft long, whilst the down main was virtually straight throughout and extended for 1,567ft. A much narrower island on the southern side was provided for suburban traffic and together with the fifteen bays helped make up a remarkable *two and three quarter miles* of platform faces. As the main through platforms could take two full sets of coaches each, it was boasted at the turn of the century that Waverley could deal with 23 trains simultaneously - more than any other British station at the time. The eight eastern bays were more or less the same length, the outer pairs having a central track for releasing engines and the inner pairs a scissors crossing for the same purpose. Waverley Bridge and its cab ramps rising at 1 in 15 from the concourse complicated matters at the western end and the seven bays had a more varied configuration. The northern one consisted of a single track with platforms either side and ended under the cab access, whilst the southern pair were similarly truncated by the cab exit. Although the middle bays came right up to the concourse, their outer ends terminated short of the others, just beyond Waverley Bridge. Each had a central release road. Two through lines were provided beyond each of the main platform tracks, the nearer ones connected to these by scissors crossings to aid shunting movements and allow departing trains to by-pass others immediately ahead of them.

Most of the platform area was covered by a vast overall roof consisting of transverse glazed gables supported on massive masonry walls and over a hundred hefty steel columns. Virtually all the station offices and amenities were contained in a large rectangular block stretching from the concourse to the east end bays. From street level the building was hardly noticeable but it presented a grand stone exterior to the platforms and was luxuriously appointed within. The booking hall had a fine mosaic floor, an abundance of wrought iron and rich Baroque stonework embellishing the walls. A dome formed the centrepiece of its lofty glazed ceiling and looked down on the octagonal booking office which was clad in superb oak cabinetwork. Waiting rooms, enquiry and reservation offices, a dining room and refreshment areas were found elsewhere in the building, whilst a couple of passageways with oak parquet floors led to the eastern bays. The suburban island had its own booking office and waiting rooms. In marked contrast to these lavish facilities, access to the station was inconvenient and unattractive. Waverley Steps descended from Princes Street and led to a lattice footbridge across the platforms with stairs to the concourse and suburban island. There were also the notorious cab ramps with their bleak pedestrian pavements, descending from Waverley Bridge The comprehensive layout was

Haymarket station stands immediately west of the tunnel from Princes Street Gardens and is still dominated by the fine Edinburgh & Glasgow Railway building, facing Haymarket Terrace. The extensive platform facilities dated from quadrupling work in the 1890s. B1 4-6-0 No.61007 KLIPSPRINGER made a punctual arrival with the 1.20pm Fife coast working from Edinburgh Waverley to Crail on 12th October 1957. Road level buildings at various angles were an indication of the complex junction of Haymarket Terrace, West Maitland Street and Dalry Road, immediately outside the station.

Haymarket station was the finest building on the Edinburgh & Glasgow Railway. The former terminus was a dignified classical design in stone, displaying perfect symmetry and excellent craftsmanship. Slightly projecting wings had pronounced quoins (corner stones) whilst a subtle cornice and low parapet hid the roofline. A neat portico supported on simple columns sheltered the entrance and a proud clock with a round hood relieved the otherwise horizontal and vertical lines of the structure. The listed building with its thoughtfully improved forecourt is seen here on 10th June 1994. Photograph Paul Anderson.

Traces of snow lingered at Haymarket on 6th February 1965 as St. Margarets B1 4-6-0 No.61350 drew in on time with the 11.50am special from Hawick for the Scotland -v- Wales Rugby International at Murrayfield. Another local special was brought in by V2 2-6-2 No.60846. Overnight excursions from Wales were routed into Edinburgh Princes Street but arrived four hours late owing to the theft of signal wires south of Carlisle. They returned to the Principality overnight on Saturday and Sunday. Haymarket's grandiose clock provided an interesting contrast to the ample yet rather dull North British canopies.

completed by three carriage sidings next to the Market, fruit and newspaper bays adjacent to Market Street and a spacious goods depot in the south east corner of the site. An impressive 228 points were incorporated in the trackwork and train movements were controlled by 290 signals. West and East cabins were situated at the respective station throats and huge signal bridges stood next to them. North and South boxes were centrally placed on the edge of the through tracks and a fifth cabin was located on the suburban island. A staff of 500 worked at Waverley.

At long last the North British made an impact on the Edinburgh skyline, and it was a very dramatic one. The company wanted a prestigious hotel to complement its rebuilt station and a site near the General Post Office at the opposite corner of North Bridge and Princes Street was selected. For five years the massive square block gradually took shape above the station and the North British Hotel finally opened on 15th October 1902. Guests were variously treated to views of Calton Hill, Arthur's Seat, Castle Rock and the Scott Monument. There was accommodation for 400, including spacious bachelor suites let by the year for 'gentlemen residing in the city'. Ground floor public rooms included the Palm Lounge, Ballroom, Coffee Lounge, Supper Room and Reading Room. All were elaborately decorated with mahogany panelling, silk wall hangings, plaster friezes and Renaissance ceilings. As a landmark it was superb and on a clear day the tower could be seen from the Forth Bridge approaches with Arthur's Seat as a backdrop. It also complemented the monuments of Calton Hill perfectly when viewed along Princes Street.

During the ample Edwardian years Waverley dealt with up to 1,400 trains a day at the height of the summer timetable, including over 100 expresses and 30 to 40 holiday specials. In 1912 there were 350 suburban services in and out of the station a day, including 36 on the South Side circle, 56 to and from Musselburgh

Seen from the Caledonian overbridge carrying tracks from Dalry Junction to Granton, B1 4-6-0 No.61132 passed Haymarket Central Junction with the ten coach 1.14pm rugby special from Dysart to Edinburgh Haymarket on 6th February 1965. Murrayfield stadium is beyond Haymarket shed, which is just visible through the mist in the right background. The concrete coaling tower was being dismantled at the time. Another famous sporting venue, Tynecastle, home of Hearts FC, is beyond the factories on the left, off Gorgie Road. Haymarket Central Junction marked the divergence of the Southside Suburban Circle (behind the train) but the box also controlled various crossovers and access to the motive power depot.

Though renowned for its more glamorous duties, Haymarket provided engines for secondary main line passenger services too, together with stopping trains in Fife, and its sizeable stud of 4-4-0s was mainly used for these turns. On the misty afternoon of 26th March 1955, D11s Nos. 62685 MALCOLM GRAEME and 62678 LUCKIE MUCKLEBACKIT stood silently in the gloom at the north end of the shed. In the background a couple of D49s were equally moribund, that on the right being No.62705 LANARKSHIRE. Main line diesels, including the legendary Deltics, were serviced at Haymarket from the early 1960s and the facilities closed to steam in 1963. It is now a Sprinter depot, having lost its diesel loco allocation.

and 72 on each of the North Leith and Leith Central routes. The cheap weekly zone tickets allowing unlimited travel from 25 local stations introduced during 1906 to counter tramway competition kept these services buoyant. No less than 50 trains connected Edinburgh and Glasgow via Falkirk or Bathgate between 4.30am and 9.15pm. Most of the former were composed of the latest corridor bogie stock including refreshment cars offering breakfast, dinner or afternoon tea as appropriate. Despite this ample provision, passengers often found it difficult to obtain seats. The old 'Fife and North' expresses which departed from the east end and were ferried across the Firth of Forth were no more, and had been replaced by a vastly increased service following the opening of the Forth Bridge. There were seven fast trains to Aberdeen and four 'Highland Expresses' to Inverness with through Great North of Scotland Railway coaches for Elgin. Overnight excursions from England arrived before the daily routine got underway and their passengers provided good business for Waverley's tea rooms, but the highlight of the morning was undoubtedly the departure of the 10.00am 'Flying Scotsman' for London King's Cross. A Waverley route express for London St. Pancras via Carlisle followed at 10.30am. Most platforms were dedicated to particular services - East Coast trains left from the north side of the main island or east end bay No.1 for example, whilst Waverley route departures used the south side through line or bay No.8. Intermediate bays on the east side were reserved for local trains to Leith, Musselburgh, Dalkeith, Glencorse, Penicuik, Polton, Peebles, Macmerry, Gifford, Haddington, Gullane, North Berwick and Dunbar. West end platforms were divided more or less equally between the Glasgow and Forth Bridge routes, whilst the suburban island accommodated excursions, specials and the occasional express between its usual humdrum duties. The innermost through roads beyond the main platform tracks were occasionally used for non-stop trains, but their main purpose was for stock movements. The outermost lines were frequently employed for stabling specials between duties.

Just after the Grouping of 1923, Waverley was handling about a thousand trains a day and had just about recovered from the disruption caused by World War I. Four station pilots were necessary to transfer carriages between trains, attach fish vans, and remove restaurant and sleeping cars for servicing. One of the busiest periods was from 3.00am to 4.30am when overnight expresses from London to the north arrived and sleepers for Fort William, Inverness, Aberdeen and Lossiemouth had to be marshalled. Through coaches from Penzance to Aberdeen via Leicester Central were also dealt with at this time. Between 6.00am and 7.30am nocturnal services from London King's Cross, London St. Pancras and Bristol arrived. A Leeds express came in about 1.45pm and the day trains from King's Cross and St. Pancras, including the 'Flying Scotsman' were received from 6.00pm to 7.30pm. Early afternoon workings from London arrived between 8.45pm and 9.45pm, concluding the main business of the day. Meanwhile, suburban operations had been made a little easier by through workings such as Glasgow Hyndland to Leith Central and Glasgow Queen Street to North Berwick and Gullane. Inner suburban traffic was al-

WEST END	EAST END
4.00pm Glasgow Queen Street	4.03pm Haddington/North Berwick
4.05pm Leith Central (via Suburban Inner Circle)	4.10pm Carlisle
4.10pm Stirling	4.13pm Leith Central
4.17pm Corstorphine	4.18pm Musselburgh
4.25pm Aberdeen	4.40pm Leith Central;
4.27pm Glasgow Queen Street (all stations)	4.45pm Musselburgh
	4.46pm North Leith (steam car)
4.31pm Perth	5.00pm Gullane/North Berwick
4.45pm Leith Central (via Suburban Inner Circle)	5.03pm Gifford
	5.06pm Galashiels (via Peebles)
4.46pm Corstorphine	5.08pm Glencorse
5.00pm Dundee Tay Bridge (via Crail)	5.11pm Leith Central
	5.12pm Leeds (ex Glasgow Queen Street)
5.05pm Glasgow Queen Street (all stations)	5.15pm Penicuik
5.07pm Dundee Tay Bridge	5.21pm Musselburgh
5.10pm Suburban Inner Circle	5.24pm Galashiels
5.13pm Corstorphine	5.25pm North Leith (steam car)
5.15pm Dalmeny (via Kirkliston - steam car)	5.30pm Haddington/Dunbar
	5.33pm Polton
5.20pm Duddingston	5.38pm Dalkeith
5.31pm Polmont	5.41pm Leith Central
5.35pm Stirling	5.46pm Musselburgh
5.40pm Corstorphine	5.48pm Leith Central
5.45pm Leith Central (via Suburban Inner Circle)	5.50pm Carlisle
5.55pm Thornton	

**WAVERLEY DEPARTURES
4.00pm - 6.00pm May 1930**

In BR days Haymarket shed (64B) was almost exclusively a main line passenger depot, providing motive power for expresses as far as Aberdeen, Glasgow, Newcastle and York. In 1955 its allocation of 80 engines clearly reflected this, for there were no less than 37 Pacifics, of classes A1, A2, A3 and A4. The remaining tender locos comprised four V2 2-6-2s, nine B1 4-6-0s and sixteen 4-4-0s, of classes D11 and D49. There were also tank engines for empty carriage workings and local yard shunting - three V3 2-6-2Ts, five J83 0-6-0Ts and a pair of J88 0-6-0Ts. There were also two J36 0-6-0s for the South Queensferry goods. Typical of the top link machines was appropriately-named class A2/1 Pacific No.60509 WAVERLEY, in magnificent repose on 2nd October 1954.

ready declining, but this was balanced by an increasing demand for middle distance services. Some idea of Waverley's operations can be gleaned from the weekday departures for May 1930 (Opposite))

In 1958 no less than 27 expresses left Waverley on weekdays, in addition to the fast diesel service to Glasgow Queen Street which ran approximately hourly. The London King's Cross trains were the most numerous and still carried a lot of prestige. In order, they were 'The Fair Maid' at 8.30am (ex-Perth), 'The Elizabethan' at 9.45am (non-stop), 'The Flying Scotsman' at 10.00am, an unnamed 11.00am departure, 'The Queen of Scots' Pullman via Leeds at 12.05pm (ex-Glasgow Queen Street), 'The Heart of Midlothian' at 1.30pm (ex-Perth), 'The Talisman' at 4.00pm, and 'The Night Scotsman' sleeper at 10.50pm. 'The Aberdonian' sleeper from Aberdeen to London King's Cross called but did not pick up passengers. There was also 'The North Briton' at 5.15pm (Glasgow Queen Street to Leeds Central) and two trains to London St. Pancras via Carlisle and Leeds City - 'The Waverley' at 10.05am and a sleeper at 9.45pm. Twelve expresses travelled north including Aberdeen departures at 7.30am, 10.00am, 2.15pm, 4.17pm and 6.45pm. The others ran to Perth at 7.40am, 10.12am (also to Inverness), 2.00pm, 2.50pm ('The Fair Maid' ex-London King's Cross), 4.00pm (also to Inverness), 6.55pm and 10.55pm (also to Inverness). Finally there were through trains to Glasgow Queen Street at 4.55am (ex-Colchester), 1.50pm ('The North Briton' ex-Leeds Central), 6.45pm (ex-London King's Cross) and 8.00pm ('The Queen of Scots' ex-London King's Cross).

Weekday departures from Waverley between 4.00pm and 6.00pm during June 1958 were significantly different to those of 1930. The growth in medium distance residential traffic was reflected by the increase in trains to Glasgow and over the Forth Bridge from the west end, whilst the demise of several branch line passenger services had seen a marked reduction

WEST END	EAST END
4.00pm Glasgow Queen Street ('The Talisman')	4.00pm London King's Cross
4.00pm Perth	4.05pm Dunbar
4.17pm Aberdeen (ex Kings Cross)	4.10pm Hawick
4.20pm Dundee	4.15pm Mussleburgh
4.25pm Stirling	4.21pm Galashiels (via Peebles)
4.30pm Glasgow Queen Street	4.30pm North Berwick
4.35pm Glasgow Queen Street	4.44pm Mussleburgh
4.40pm Suburban Inner Circle	4.58pm Suburban Outer Circle
4.43pm Corstorphine	5.05pm Galashiels (via Peebles)
5.03pm Thornton Junction (via Dunfermline)	5.11pm St. Boswells/Kelso
5.10pm St. Andrews (via Crail)	5.15pm Leeds (The 'North Briton' ex-Glasgow Queen St.)
5.15pm Glasgow Queen Street	5.18pm North Berwick
5.15pm Corstorphine	5.21pm Mussleburgh
5.23pm Suburban Inner Circle	5.27pm Rosewell & Hawthornden
5.25pm Dundee	5.38pm Dunbar
5.29pm Thornton Junction (via Dunfermline)	5.45pm Musselburgh
5.35pm Dundee	5.52pm Carlile
5.40pm Corstorphine	
5.45pm Suburban Inner Circle	
5.50pm Corstorphine	**WAVERLEY DEPARTURES**
5.54pm Glasgow Queen Street	**4.00pm-6.00pm June 1958**
6.00pm Glasgow Queen Street	

Left:- On 19th March 1960, B1 4-6-0 No.61221 SIR ALEXANDER ERSKINE-HILL passed Haymarket Central Junction with the 3.43pm from Edinburgh Waverley to Ladybank, comprising mainly Gresley vehicles. Meanwhile Thompson A1 Pacific No.60161 NORTH BRITISH came off Haymarket shed and headed towards Waverley for a stint on express passenger work. The Southside Suburban line veers off in the foreground and the Caledonian overbridge is beyond the train.

Below:- At Broxburn Junction, a mile south of Winchburgh tunnel on the Edinburgh & Glasgow main line, the mineral branches to Niddry Castle and Broxburn diverged. They both served shale oil works, the latter continuing to Drumshoreland on the Bathgate route. With a sprinkling of snow on the ground, Haymarket J36 0-6-0 No.65288 pottered about at Broxburn Junction on 26th December 1962 with the 'Ferry Goods' which, as its name indicated, also ventured down to South Queensferry.

of activity at the east end. (table page 41) In many ways Waverley has changed little since 1902, but this is a mixed blessing. The setting, with Princes Street Gardens, the Scott Monument, Castle Rock and the Old Town peering down over the west end is as spectacular as ever of course, and the overall roof and canopies are intact. A wealth of classical detail can still be discovered in panelling, stonework and metal columns, although the station badly needed a repaint in 1994. Even the former booking hall retains its splendour, despite wholesale changes to the interior of the main building. The hotel, now in private ownership and rechristened 'The Balmoral' is an essential part of the Edinburgh skyline, on a par with Calton Hill. On the minus side, access to Waverley has improved not one iota, with vehicles presenting a constant danger to pedestrians in the fume-laden taxi ramps and Waverley Steps becoming a dark and sinister place to many passengers at night. Constant pleas for escalators up to Princes Street have been ignored. As a

Boxing Day 1962, and J36 No.65288 collected an empty wagon at derelict Broxburn Shale Oil Works. In Great Britain, bitumen-rich shales were restricted to the Midland Valley of Scotland and they were mined, crushed and heated in retorts to yield oil. This distillation process was relatively expensive and was to succumb readily to competition from foreign oilfields. It also created copious amounts of waste which was dumped in huge flat-topped mounds, and several of these disfigured the Winchburgh - Pumpherston area. One of the unsightly monuments to this particularly messy industry can be seen on the left. The line to Broxburn continues across the Union Canal in the middle distance.

result of electrification, Edinburgh continues to enjoy Britain's finest expresses, the InterCity 225s maintaining a 150 year tradition. Services from the west end have continued to expand, with 31 departures on weekdays between 16.00 and 18.00 in 1994, a train every four minutes compared with one every five and a half minutes in 1958. It is a very different picture at the east end following the virtual annihilation of local services and the demise of the Waverley route. This part of the station is now a lonely barn of a place, largely given over to car parking, and just three King's Cross expresses together with three North Berwick electric multiple units on their way out disturbed the haunts of the old suburban trains during the same two hour period.

The Oakbank Oil Co. Ltd. operated a 2ft 6in gauge electrified system, some two miles in length, serving shale mines north of Winchburgh and a refinery east of the village. Loco No.4, a steeple cab built by English Electric in 1927, stood near its shed in a leafy setting at Winchburgh Refinery on 12th May 1956. The line closed early in 1961.

Philipstoun was one of the less successful stations on the Edinburgh & Glasgow route. It opened in 1885 and served isolated farms and dwellings such as Mounthooly, Champfleurie and Merrylees, as well as the tiny village itself. Passenger services ceased in 1951 but goods facilities were maintained until 1964 - though merely as an unstaffed public siding from May 1955. Class 5 4-6-0 No.45084 passed the remains of the station with the 1.26pm from Stirling to Edinburgh Waverley on 24th April 1965. The view was taken from an overbridge carrying the lane from Old Philipstoun to Philipstoun, which can be seen in the distance. Three miles away, the 500ft Bonnytoun ridge overlooks Linlithgow Loch to the left and drops down to Bo'ness on the Firth of Forth to the right.

Edinburgh & Glasgow stations were very durable and Linlithgow retains its original dour stone building, albeit with a few North British appendages, as Haymarket B1 4-6-0 No.61245 MURRAY OF ELIBANK called with the 2.48pm from Crail to Glasgow Queen Street via the Forth Bridge on 16th July 1960. Apart from a couple of BR standard carriages, the seven coach train was composed of 'Silver Jubilee' stock. These vehicles were stored during the war in anticipation of the reinstatement of the service, but this never happened. Instead they were employed on medium distance services, occasionally still in silver livery at first, and provided spacious and comfortable accommodation for local passengers. Just quarter of a mile from the station, away to the left, the fine 15th century palace where Mary Queen of Scots was born stands in the precincts on the edge of Linlithgow Loch. To the right the ground rises towards Parkley Hill and the chimney belongs to a hospital on the lower slopes. Linlithgow still has passenger trains, but the goods yard closed on 28th February 1966.

Ex-LMS class 5 No.45127 and B1 4-6-0 No.61347 basked in spring sunshine at St. Margarets on 23rd April 1966 as several of the problem-ridden Clayton Type 1 diesels appropriately lurked in the shadows. The depot was very much on the decline and the days when a sizeable proportion of its huge complement had to be outstationed at South Leith, Craigentinny and other sidings at the weekends were just a memory. It closed on 1st May 1967 with the end of Scottish Region steam and the soot-caked yet still dignified buildings were cleared away. This constricted site, hemmed in by tenement-lined roads and the main line, has since been redeveloped. The old part of the depot, on the up side of the through tracks, now forms part of the Meadowbank Stadium complex, while the four and a half acre site on the down side now houses an office block.

Craigentinny carriage sidings were established in 1913 on open ground near Restalrig, about two and a half miles east of Waverley. Countless rakes of spruced-up main line stock were drawn out of the depot by St. Margarets tank or goods engines over the years, and the tradition continued on 21st August 1964. Standard 2-6-4T No.80122 waited for the road as a Gloucester twin, forming the 3.40pm from Musselburgh to Edinburgh Waverley, rattled past. Portobello formed the skyline and the appropriately named Fishwives Causeway ran behind the wall on the left in this view from a footbridge between Portobello Road and Mountcastle estate. Unlike Haymarket and St. Margarets sheds, Craigentinny was never a magnet for enthusiasts in steam days, yet ironically it is now Edinburgh's main traction depot and has housed HSTs since 1978, and class 91 electric locos with their 225 coaching sets since 1991.

Between Portobello and Joppa there was a spread of carriage sidings on the north side of the main line and these could be seen from Hope Lane bridge on 16th July 1962 as class 5 4-6-0 No.45484 joined the East Coast route at Portobello East Junction with a mixed rake of ex-LMS and LNER stock. This was a Glasgow Fair Monday excursion from Blantyre and Hamilton to Portobello and Edinburgh Waverley. Its somewhat unlikely approach to the capital, from the east, was made possible by leaving the Caledonian line at Slateford, joining the Southside Suburban tracks at Craiglockhart and reaching the Waverley route via Niddrie West Junction. The embankment and plate girder bridge in the middle distance are part of the Lothian Lines and Joppa station is hidden by steam from the class 5.

On 3rd April 1961, V3 2-6-2T No.67649 was making a determined effort with the 4.05pm local from Edinburgh Waverley to Dunbar as it breasted a minor summit at Newhailes on the three mile stretch between Joppa and Inveresk. Modern corridor stock was provided for this unassuming service. The Lothian Lines connection from the East Coast main line climbed away on the left and the Musselburgh branch came in beyond the train.

A1 Pacific No.60116 HAL O' THE WYND drifted down the 1 in 300 from Prestonpans and approached Inveresk with an Edinburgh-bound freight on 21st August 1964. The photograph was taken from Crookston Road bridge and clearly shows the undulating coastal plain crossed by the northern end of the North British main line. Barbachlaw Farm and Wallyford in the middle distance lead the eye to Falside Hill which rises to 474ft on the right. These quiet fields were the site of a bloody conflict in 1547 when the Earl of Hertford defeated the Scots at the Battle of Pinkie, as a result of which the infant Mary Queen of Scots was sent to France for twelve years.

Prestonpans still had its neat wooden buildings with slate roofs and plenty of well maintained flower beds on 28th August 1960 as Gresley A3 Pacific No.60085 MANNA ambled in with the 3.48pm local from Edinburgh Waverley to Berwick, formed of four non-corridor coaches. On the left is a poster, for the centenary of far-off Royal Albert Bridge at Saltash, based on a famous Cuneo painting. In 1745 the gentle slopes away to the right saw another great battle, Prestonpans, where Bonnie Prince Charlie and his Highlanders crushed the army of Sir John Cope in the last of the Jacobite rebellions.

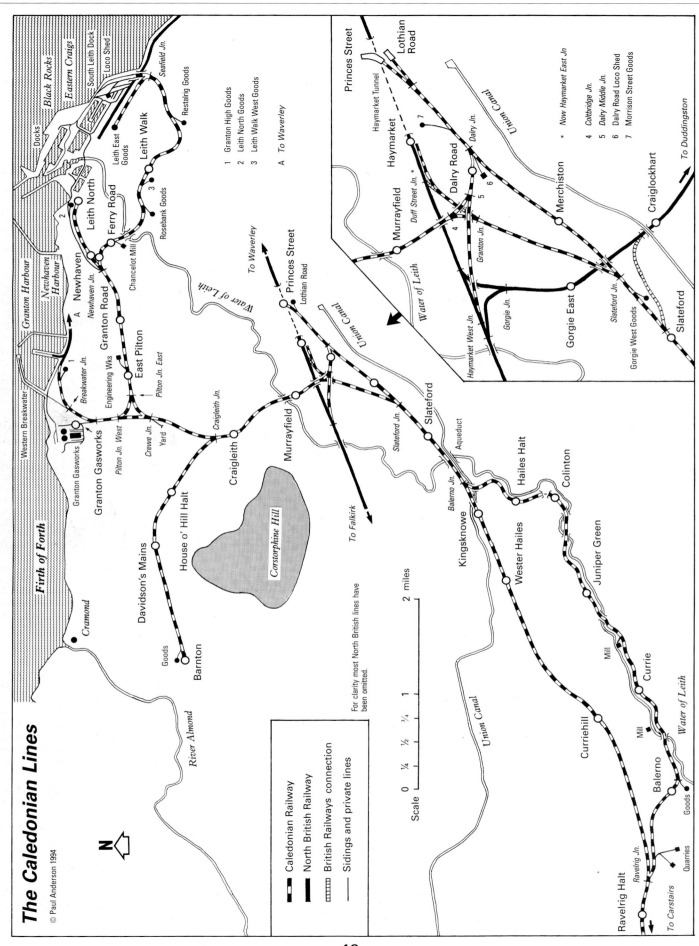

The Caledonian Lines

© Paul Anderson 1994

N

Firth of Forth

Docks
Black Rocks
Eastern Craigs
South Leith Dock
Loco Shed
Seafield Jn.
Restalrig Goods

Leith East Goods
Leith Walk
Leith North
Ferry Road
Rosebank Goods
Chancelot Mill
Newhaven Jn.
Newhaven

1 Granton High Goods
2 Leith North Goods
3 Leith Walk West Goods
A To Waverley

Granton Harbour
Newhaven Harbour
Western Breakwater
Breakwater Jn.
Granton Gasworks
Engineering Wks
East Pilton
Pilton Jn. East
Pilton Jn. West
Crewe Jn.
Yard

Granton Road
Water of Leith
To Waverley
Princes Street
Lothian Road
Union Canal

Craigleith Jn.
Craigleith
Murrayfield
Corstorphine Hill
To Falkirk

House o' Hill Halt
Davidson's Mains

Cramond
River Almond

Goods
Barnton

Slateford Jn.
Slateford
Aqueduct
Balerno Jn.
Kingsknowe
Wester Hailes
Hailes Halt
Colinton
Juniper Green

Union Canal

Curriehill
Currie
Mill
Mill
Balerno
Goods
Water of Leith

Ravelrig Halt
Ravelrig Jn.
Quarries
To Carstairs

Scale
0   ¼   ½   ¾   1   2 miles

For clarity most North British lines have been omitted.

Princes Street
Lothian Road
Haymarket Tunnel
Haymarket
Murrayfield
Now Haymarket East Jn
Coltbridge Jn.
Dalry Middle Jn.
Dalry Road Loco Shed
Morrison Street Goods

* Now Haymarket East Jn
4 Coltbridge Jn.
5 Dalry Middle Jn.
6 Dalry Road Loco Shed
7 Morrison Street Goods

Dalry Jn.
Dalry Road
Duff Street Jn. *
Granton Jn.
Haymarket West Jn.
Water of Leith
Union Canal
Merchiston
Craiglockhart
To Duddingston
Gorgie Jn.
Gorgie East
Gorgie West Goods
Slateford Jn.
Slateford

Caledonian Railway
North British Railway
British Railways connection
Sidings and private lines

Chapter 3

The Caledonian

In this late 1950s view, the huge end screen at Princes Street was illuminated by afternoon sunshine and still looked magnificent despite the accumulated grime. Fine woodwork matched the massive pillars which finished off the side walls, whilst intricate motifs in decorative iron added interesting detail. The top of the screen was fringed with fussy metalwork including minaret-like columns. Ex-North British class D30 4-4-0 No.62426 CUDDIE HEADRIGG waited with a departure for Stirling via Polmont as Fairburn 2-6-4T No.42269 stood in the siding immediately east of the train shed. This particular D30 was regularly employed on Stirling - Princes Street services in the 1950s and on at least one occasion the train consisted of just two non-corridor coaches. No.62426 was not withdrawn until 1960, being one of the last two 'Scotts' to survive. Photograph G.M. Staddon, Neville Stead Collection.

Little more than eighteen months after the Edinburgh & Glasgow and North British began to run services from Waverley, another trunk route reached the Scottish capital. The infant Caledonian Railway had its share of English traffic from the outset, despite being dogged by dishonest management and shambolic finances during its early years. There was also a determined bid for Edinburgh - Glasgow passengers resulting in the ruinous price war noted earlier. Like the North British, the Caledonian's main Edinburgh station was a poor show and the replacement was little better. Again, as at Waverley, the final version was at last worthy of the city and the hotel became a local landmark. Gradually the company established a sizeable network around Edinburgh, with

lines to Granton and Leith docks, several suburban stations and a couple of very picturesque branches. The final fling was an ambitious attempt to provide a circular route through Leith involving numerous viaducts and an underground section below the city centre, but this proved abortive. Most of the system has been abandoned and grandiose Princes Street terminus has largely disappeared. However, many of the former trackbeds survive as walkways and the original main line approach is now electrified, seeing some Glasgow-bound InterCity 225s which have made their way up the former North British route from Berwick.

THE MAIN LINE
Serious interest in a railway from Central Scotland to England was expressed

in 1836, spurred on by the emerging trunk routes from London to Birmingham and Birmingham to Lancashire. After various surveys and increasing pressure for the link, a meeting to discuss the proposed Caledonian Railway was held in London during 1844, by which time the North British and Glasgow & South Western routes were also being promoted. The Caledonian received its Act for the Glasgow - Carlisle line, together with a branch from Carstairs to Lothian Road in Edinburgh, on 31st July 1845. In common with several other early main lines, construction work across the harsh Southern Uplands proceeded quite rapidly and the Carlisle to Beattock section opened on 10th September 1847 with stagecoaches providing connections to and from Edinburgh. The remaining track - including

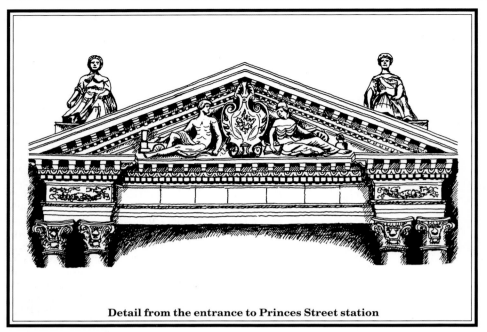

Detail from the entrance to Princes Street station

Hill and Gogar Burn to Ravelrig. Currie station (five miles from Edinburgh) followed, midway along the much easier 1 in 143 descent to Slateford station (renamed Kings Knowes on 1st January 1853 - eventually becoming Kingsknowe - and three miles from Lothian Road). A skew bridge across the Union Canal followed almost immediately and the line was then faced with the Water of Leith in its incised valley. This obstacle was conquered by a rugged fourteen arch stone viaduct, alongside the elegant canal aqueduct which was at a slightly higher level, the railway having descended at 1 in 102 from Kingsknowe. Another skew bridge over the main Lanark Road was followed by the second Slateford station (opened on 1st January 1853 and two miles from Edinburgh) then a level stretch took the Caledonian past Merchiston. A slight rise at 1 in 400 and a short drop at 1 in 126 brought the line into Lothian Road terminus.

On 9th April 1847 there was glowing optimism when the foundation stone for the magnificent new Edinburgh station was laid. The ceremony was performed by the Grand Lodge of Scotland, his Grace the Duke of Athole, Grand Master Mason, watched by the Lord Provost and magistrates of the City of Edinburgh, together with Caledonian Railway directors. William Tite had designed a fine Italianate structure with a 370ft facade consisting of three main blocks rising above an impressive colonnade. The

that between Carstairs and Lothian Road - began to carry trains on 15th February 1848, but it was a muted start devoid of celebrations, reflecting the company's worsening financial plight.

From Carstairs the line climbed northwards across bleak moorland on the western edge of the Pentland Hills with gradients as steep as 1 in 97. At Cobbinshaw summit in the shadow of 988ft Pearie Law the descent to Edinburgh began, initially at 1 in 100 down the Bog Burn valley through Harburn, then over a viaduct spanning Linhouse Water. Just before Midcalder the gradient eased to 1 in 120 and small settlements became more common, in marked contrast to the sparsely settled country so far. At Midcalder station (originally Kirknewton and ten miles from Lothian Road) the Caledonian dipped below 500ft and ran on a hillside between Dalmahoy

21st October 1963, and a wet autumn evening reflected the gloom precipitated by the impending demise of Princes Street station. Class 5 4-6-0 No.45476 waited at platform 4 with the 5.18pm to Glasgow Central and sister loco No.45214 gently blew off steam at the head of the 5.32pm service to Stirling. The Edinburgh & Glasgow main line in its tunnels between Princes Street Gardens and Haymarket passed directly beneath the Caledonian terminus, approximately under the first three coaches of the Glasgow train.

Dank and misty weather masked the grand terminus as class 5 No.44978 left Princes Street with the 4.22pm for Perth on 29th February 1964. The carriage sidings with their low platforms for cleaners were well occupied in the left background. Far more prominent was the large Caledonian signal box which had a locking frame with 156 levers controlling all traffic in and around the station. Since closure the main line formation from Dalry Road to Morrison Street has been converted into Edinburgh's West Approach Road, whilst Lothian Road goods depot has been replaced by the Sheraton Hotel. Although all traces of the platforms have been eradicated, Princes Street lives on in the form of the Caledonian Hotel, which remains virtually unchanged externally.

a more stable footing. Passenger trains during these early years were in the hands of 2-2-2s with 6ft driving wheels, no less than 58 of these machines having been delivered by 1850. Connor 8ft 2-2-2s were introduced in 1859 and 2-4-0s followed during the 1860s. A pale blue precursor of the famous Caley livery was used on passenger engines.

PRINCES STREET

With traffic increasing generally and the prospect of more local passenger services, the Caledonian decided to replace its Lothian Road facilities with a new station on nearby Princes Street. An approach line diverged from the existing tracks just short of Grove Road bridge and descended below a big metal span carrying Morrison Street. No grandiose claims were made for the proposed terminus this time, and when it opened, on 2nd May 1870, the edifice lived up to expectations. It was a parallelogram in plan, roughly 500ft long and 100ft wide at its broadest. A shallow gabled timber roof partially covered two main and one ancillary platform and ended in a large screen overlooking the entrance block. Overshadowed by the Castle and elegant buildings in Lothian Road, it was only a modest addition to the city - though not unpleasant to look at. The squat transverse wooden structure faced a large forecourt near the junc-

building would have made a handsome contribution to the city's fabric but it progressed no further than the foundation stone. Instead, the lack of funds resulted in a temporary station of limited architectural merit and even more basic facilities. Incredibly, there was just a single track approach which split into three lines, one of them serving a solitary platform sheltered by an overall roof 180ft long by 54ft wide. There was a range of buildings on the south east side but the only concession to classical styling was a weak pediment finishing off the inner end of the train shed.

Although the line was designed for fast running there were no expresses at first and speeds were modest. In April 1848 just five trains a day departed from Lothian Road - at 6.50am, 11.15am, 1.30pm, 5.00pm and 9.15pm, all but the early afternoon one travelling through to Carlisle. The 9.15pm mail took four hours fifteen minutes to reach the Border town at an average of about 24mph, yet even this performance outshone the 5.00pm all stations 'Parliamentary' which needed nearly six hours (compared with ninety minutes for direct expresses today). Nevertheless the Caledonian route soon became popular, securing Royal Mail traffic from March 1848 and offering expresses to London, Birmingham, Manchester and Liverpool from the following May. By the close of 1849 the company finances had plunged into a state of utter chaos and this was hardly helped by an all out attempt to woo Edinburgh - Glasgow customers with very low fares despite the roundabout route. The 1851 Exhibi-

tion in London boosted long distance traffic and by this time a new Board of Directors was beginning to put the railway on

Dalry Road motive power depot occupied a cramped triangular site between the main line, the spur to Coltbridge Junction and Dalry Cemetery. It was overlooked by factories on two sides and bordered by Coffin Lane to the south west, just to add to the dour nature of the surroundings. The original two-road shed was supplemented by a similar structure which, rather surprisingly, replaced the turntable; afterwards engines had to use the facilities just outside Princes Street. A large four-track shed with a gabled roof was added in the early 1900s. Duties included Carlisle, Glasgow and Perth trains, suburban services to Barnton, Balerno and Leith, and dock shunting at Leith and Granton. In 1959 its allocation included nine ex-LMS class 5 4-6-0s, one mixed traffic 2-6-0, three 2-6-4Ts and an 0-6-0T. Ex-Caledonian locos comprised one 4-4-0, four 0-4-4Ts, an 0-6-0T and six 0-6-0s. Seven ex-North British 0-6-0s were also on the books. Seen from Dundee Street bridge on 29th February 1964, class 5 No.44994 passed Dalry Road with the 12.06pm from Edinburgh Princes Street to Kingsknowe as Nos.45360 and 44953 of the same class stood in the sidings. The West Approach Road now occupies the whole of this site, the shed having closed in October 1965.

Merchiston station, a mile and a quarter out of Princes Street, opened on 1st July 1882 to serve a growing suburb. This became a densely populated district, as shown by the four storey tenements on the right in Harrison Gardens and the five storey blocks on Harrison Road in the distance. The cottages in Primrose Terrace on the left are almost rural by comparison. In keeping with current Caledonian practice, the platform buildings had big low pitched roofs extended as wide canopies, supported on decorative brackets. The walkways in the foreground led to Shandon Place and Ashley Terrace. On 16th July 1962 Fairburn 2-6-4T No.42172 stormed out of Merchiston with the 5.37pm from Edinburgh Princes Street to Lanark - vestibuled coaches were in common use on local trains by this time through the run-down of non-corridor stock, a result of the influx of diesel multiple units. The station closed at the same time as Princes Street, but the scene is little changed apart from the lack of track or railway structures, and the formation is now a footpath.

tion of King's Stables and Lothian Road and it had a very low pitched slate roof sprouting neat chimneys. A substantial canopy slightly higher than the eaves was supported on big decorative brackets and sported balustrades and a large central clock with an ornate surround. Goods traffic was concentrated at the old Lothian

On 29th February 1964 Black 5 4-6-0 No.44952 rushed across Slateford viaduct with the 2.14pm from Carstairs to Edinburgh Princes Street which included through coaches from Manchester Victoria. The Union Canal aqueduct is on the left and Inglis Green Road runs beneath the furthermost arches of both structures. Shortly afterwards the train passed the site of one of Edinburgh's shortest-lived stations. During 1890 the International Industrial Exhibition was held on a large area of land bordering the railway midway between Merchiston and Slateford and it was served by a short spur off the main line. A single platform was provided from 1st May to 3rd November of that year and it enjoyed a very frequent service from Princes Street and Leith.

Road terminus but further growth in passenger services soon rendered Princes Street station just as inadequate as its predecessor; it was famously condemned as a 'wooden shanty'. On 16th June 1890 a fierce blaze consumed much of the train shed as well as several coaches. This mattered little, for a magnificent new station worthy of Edinburgh had already been planned and a contractor appointed.

Work began on the new Princes Street in autumn 1890 after the charred remains of the 'wooden shanty' had been cleared, and most of it was available for regular services by early 1893. Of necessity, the parallelogram configuration was perpetuated but it now occupied an area 1,000ft by 230ft. This time the wedge came right up to Princes Street, the buildings at last emphasising the Caledonian's presence in the capital. Facades on Lothian Road and Rutland Street were long and low, with large round-headed windows broken by heavy transoms and mullions forming a repetitive pattern. Pairs of classical columns separated the windows and these linked a massive plinth with a more delicate parapet. Classical styling became even more pompous at the outer end of the wedge where a domed roof with a flat top was fronted with a miniature version of the *Parthenon*, overlooking three archways guarded by groups of columns topped by statues. Inside the terminus there were seven platforms varying from about 450ft to over 700ft in length and from 10ft to 20ft in width, none of them having engine release tracks however. Most of the station was protected by a superb roof nearly 850ft long springing from huge stone walls enclosing the passenger area. It consisted of transverse bays with sloping sides and prominent roof lights and was finished off with a beautiful timber screen at the outer end which was undoubtedly one of the glories of the place. The platforms ended in echelon at a fair sized concourse, dominated by an oval booking office with nine windows and overlooked by a great clock surrounded by superb woodwork forming a kind of Baroque shrine. Intricate cabinetwork and glass also featured in the numerous rooms around the concourse. These included dining rooms, an oyster bar, a first class gentlemen's waiting room, the telegraph, cab and shipping offices, a hairdressing salon, and the foreign exchange. There was also a lost property office of course, and the description of its clientele in Smellie Tarbet's 1901 *Railway Magazine* article on Princes Street is just too delightful to resist quoting;

"...here, amongst others, may be found a specimen of the much abused British domestic servant in search of a brown paper parcel containing her Sunday gown and bonnet left in the rack of a compartment in which she travelled a week ago, respecting which the want of a night out

Just east of Kingsknowe the Caledonian main line crossed the Union Canal by a fish-bellied plate girder bridge on stone abutments and Fairburn 2-6-4T No.42273 rumbled over it with the 1.23pm from Kingsknowe to Edinburgh Princes Street, on 29th February 1964. Kingsknowe station can just be seen in the background. Promoted as a means of bringing much-needed coal to Edinburgh, the Union Canal opened in May 1822.

Lothian Road frontage and some of the Rutland Street facade gained an extra four storeys, three of them fairly plan but the upper one consisting of rather complex dormer gables. In retrospect, a sad loss was most of the highly embellished narrow end of the wedge where the dome was replaced by a less spectacular curly Dutch gable. The hotel opened on 21st December 1903 and in its ninety year existence has welcomed many famous visitors including Charlie Chaplin, Laurel and Hardy, Ginger Rogers, Marlon Brando, Bob Hope, Bing Crosby and even Roy Rogers and Trigger. The room occupied by the horse does not seem to have been recorded! The Caledonian Hotel has outlasted Princes Street station and is still the venue for municipal and other functions attended by dignitaries.

When Princes Street replaced Lothian Road, expresses were still in the hands of single-wheelers and in later years these included Neilson 4-2-2 No.123 which excelled in the 1888 races from London to Edinburgh. On 9th August the engine dashed from Carlisle to Princes Street in less than an hour and three quarters with four coaches, an average of

---

has prevented her making enquiries earlier; the 'Toff' in quest of his gold-headed umbrella and cigar case, which he imagines he left in a train which arrived from the suburbs about eleven o'clock the previous evening - he's not sure where he joined it; and the old lady, who informs the attendant, in a confidential whisper, that when she arrived, in the course of the forenoon, she omitted to take away her teeth, which she had taken out on the journey and laid on the arm-rest preparatory to having a 'nap'. 'You know,' she explains with a smile, 'I always take them out before I go to sleep.'

The appearance of the concourse was helped by fine pictorial posters rather than advertisements and there were slates with chalked notices about the progress of expresses and weather conditions on other parts of the Caledonian system. Electricity was used for lighting, the supply coming from a small power station off Morrison Street served by a couple of sidings. There were five carriage sidings on the western side between the train shed and Rutland Court, whilst four short spurs terminated between the eastern wall and Lothian Road. A wide signal gantry spanned seven tracks at the outer end of the platforms and the whole approach was controlled by a cabin with 156 levers.

Just six years after it opened the appearance of the station was being drastically altered by further building work. The Caledonian wanted a hotel to rival the North British pile under construction at the other end of Princes Street and the result was a less spectacular but equally prestigious establishment. Most of the

---

Princes Street Departures 4.00pm-6.00pm May 1930

4.04pm Leith
4.10pm Barnton
4.15pm Symington (through coaches for Sheffield, Liverpool and Manchester)
4.25pm Perth
4.28pm Craigleith (workers service to Granton Gasworks)
4.37pm Leith
4.40pm Carstairs (through coaches for Ayr via Muirkirk)
4.43pm Balerno
4.50pm Glasgow Central (express with Pullman car)
5.05pm Leith
5.09pm Barnton
5.13pm Balerno
5.32pm Leith
5.35pm Carstairs (through coaches for Crewe)
5.45pm Beattock
5.49pm Barnton
5.52pm Balerno
6.00pm Glasgow Central

Princes Street Departures 4.00pm-6.00pm June 1958

4.05pm Lanark (through coaches for Liverpool)
4.23pm Perth (through coaches for Oban)
4.40pm Glasgow Central
4.43pm Leith North
4.48pm Muirkirk
5.00pm Leith North
5.17pm Glasgow Central
5.20pm Leith North
5.30pm Stirling
5.35pm Lanark (through coaches for Crewe)
5.38pm Kingsknowe
5.40pm Leith North
5.55pm Lanark
6.00pm Leith North

Fairburn 2-6-4T No.42273 had just rounded its train and was drawing into Kingsknowe before forming the 1.23pm back to Princes Street on 29th February 1964. It had arrived with the 12.57pm from Edinburgh a few minutes earlier. The station, which was originally called Slateford, had a neat little stone building with steeply pitched roofs and tall chimneys although later timber accretions somewhat spoiled its appearance. It closed on 6th July 1964 but after a vigorous campaign reopened on 1st February 1971 to serve the growing housing area nearby. Kingsknowe Golf Course and sidings for stabling coal wagons form the form the background, whilst the signal box, with its splendid finial, is prominent beyond the level crossing.

In lovely summer sunshine Standard class 5 4-6-0 No.73055 drifted past the remains of the platforms at Curriehill with the 12.30pm Glasgow Central - Edinburgh Princes Street, on 20th June 1964. The station opened on 15th February 1848 and was originally called Currie, until facilities of that name were provided on the Balerno branch nearer the village. Curriehill House, which inspired the new name, is on the hillside above the train. This was still open country when passenger and goods facilities were withdrawn on 2nd April 1951 and the landscape became fairly dramatic later on where the abrupt volcanic outcrops of Kaimes Hill and Dalmahoy Hill reared above the line. A considerable number of houses were subsequently built nearby, justifying reopening on 5th October 1987. A completely new station at Wester Hailes, a mile and three quarters miles nearer to Edinburgh and at the western end of Kingsknowe Golf Course, had opened on 11th May 1987. Again it served new development.

almost 60mph. Drummond 4-4-0s followed and the new Princes Street soon saw a succession of 'Dunalastair' 4-4-0s designed by McIntosh. Large 4-6-0s then arrived, including the mighty 'Cardean' class, with Pickersgill concluding the line of notable Caley Locomotive Superintendents. Meanwhile station pilot duties were performed by old single wheelers from Lothian Road days and a whole series of 0-4-4Ts handled local passenger services with 0-6-0s familiar on various goods workings. LMS 4-4-0s and Black 5 4-6-0s had taken over many fast and semi fast trains by Nationalisation and the latter were still around when the station closed. Diesel multiple units had displaced the 0-4-4Ts and 0-6-0s on most local services by the late 1950s but Fairburn and BR Standard 2-6-4Ts were used on main line stopping trains until the end. An interesting feature of Princes Street during the 1950s was the use of ex-LMS and BR Standard Pacifics on filling in turns from Glasgow Central, often on very mundane duties. Dalry Road shed, three quarters of a mile out of Princes Street, always had a stud of engines to handle these main line, local and goods workings but it lacked the prestige of Glasgow Polmadie and nearby Haymarket - certainly after the Grouping of 1923.

By 1900 about 180 trains were dealt with at Princes Street on weekdays, and the total swelled to well over 200 with seasonal extras and excursions at the height of summer - a far cry from 1848. A

Evening sunshine cast long shadows from the impressive stone buildings at Midcalder as Black 5 4-6-0 No.45030 paused with the 6.10pm from Edinburgh Princes Street to Glasgow Central on 5th July 1958. Note the route indicator for the Glasgow - Edinburgh route over the buffer beam. Two days later most of these workings were taken over by diesel multiple units. The station was originally called Kirknewton and has now reverted to that name. It had a sizeable goods yard which was fairly full on this occasion, but facilities were withdrawn on 18th May 1964. The remaining station on this stretch of the main line was Ravelrig platform, east of Midcalder. It opened on 4th April 1884 and latterly served the local golf club, until closed on 1st July 1920.

lifted as far as Gorgie where the upgraded Slateford - Haymarket link diverged. However the Caley approach to Edinburgh more than survived this depressing decline and was electrified on 8th July 1991.

THE BRANCHES

Even before its Edinburgh line opened, the Caledonian had ambitions to tap the lucrative shipping traffic at Granton and Leith. In 1846 it sought parliamentary approval for a line from Slateford to Granton but this was rejected. The company was back again the following year and this time an Act was obtained, but a particularly obstructive landowner frustrated the scheme and it was abandoned. Maybe this was foreseen, as the Edinburgh Station and Branches Act of 1847 also sanctioned a line from Slateford to Haymarket on the Edinburgh & Glasgow Railway. This would have enabled Caledonian goods trains to reach the docks via North Bridge and Scotland Street tunnel over the Edinburgh, Leith & Granton Railway, but it was now the turn of the Edinburgh & Glasgow to become awkward and it refused to allow a connection at Haymarket. When the mile and a quarter line opened in 1853 it gave access to several industrial sites but merely ran into a bay platform at Haymarket - so near and yet so far from the sea. Fortunately for the Caledonian, the Duke of

glimpse of the level of service provided during LMS and early BR days may be had by examining departures between 4.00pm and 6.00pm on weekdays in May 1930 and June 1958. This also gives a direct comparison with the contemporary Waverley timetable of the previous chapter. In May 1930 there was still a wide variety of local services. In May 1930 there was still a wide variety of local services, but apart from Leith these had faded away by June 1958 (*see table page 51*).

There were very few named trains out of Princes Street. In pre-war LMS times there were the Edinburgh portions of the 'Royal Scot' and 'Midday Scot', both of them carrying headboards; the Caledonian ran a 'Strathearn Express' to St. Fillans and the 'Tinto' to Moffat, but it is doubtful that these displayed their names.

By 1963 Princes Street had lost most of its suburban traffic and there was ample room for long distance services. The Beeching Report focused attention on the over-capacity of railway facilities in Edinburgh and the former Caledonian terminus had to go. Lothian Road depot, which had spent 116 years handling goods, closed on 3rd August 1964. Passenger services to Glasgow and Carlisle were still important and in order to accommodate them at Waverley a line between Slateford and Haymarket, the northern half of which had been an industrial siding for most of its long life, was adapted to take main line passenger trains. Princes Street station closed on 6th September 1965, by which time it was a slumbering giant for some of the day.

The large goods depot at Morrison Street was also somewhat superfluous when it ceased to accept consignments on 15th August 1966. Shortly afterwards the former main line through Merchiston was

Most Caledonian branches in Edinburgh were worthwhile projects but the prototype was rather a failure, at least in its early years. The Slateford - Haymarket line was meant to be a route to the docks; instead it merely provided access to a goods bay at the Edinburgh & Glasgow station after completion in 1853. Although the southern section became busy as new connections were opened, the northern part had to wait for 111 years before graduating from an industrial siding to a through route. Prior to the demise of Princes Street it was rebuilt as the Duff Street spur, enabling trains from Glasgow Central and Carlisle to reach Waverley. This new role began on 7th September 1964. The new trackwork was prominent on the right as Black 5 4-6-0 No.44867 headed the 1.28pm football special from Edinburgh Waverley to Falkirk Grahamston, past Duff Street Junction, on 6th February 1965. Commandeered after attention at Cowlairs Works, the engine was based at 9B Stockport Edgeley shed.

Dalry Road station was on the curve close to Dalry Junction where the 1864 spur to Coltbridge Junction left the main line, although it actually opened on 2nd July 1900, long after the Leith passenger service began. It was a grimy place, surrounded by factories and adjacent to Dalry Road motive power depot. Although the Leith North passenger services were provided by diesel multiple units from 1958, the branch would revert to steam traction for important rugby matches at Murrayfield in order to provide extra seating capacity. One such occasion was 19th March 1960 when Scotland played England, and J39 0-6-0 No.64946 was in charge of the 1.40pm Edinburgh Princes Street - Leith North at Dalry Road prior to the kick-off. B1 4-6-0 No.61398 was at the shed coaling stage on the right.

V3 2-6-2T No.67624 with a sizeable rake of non-corridor stock steamed out of Dalry Road forming the 1.10pm from Leith North to Edinburgh Princes Street on 19th March 1960 before the Scotland -v- England Rugby International at Murrayfield. Despite its awkward site the station was quite substantial, consisting of a long and broad island platform with a timber building featuring big canopies finished off with decorative valances. There was little finesse about the structure, however, and the Caledonian did not repeat the attractive style recently provided on the Cathcart Circle in Glasgow. The general gloom was being assisted by a couple of 0-6-0s, one propelling wagons up to the stage at Dalry Road shed and the other taking on coal.

Buccleuch wanted some competition at Granton and approached the railway company in 1856 with a plan to jointly promote a mineral line from the Haymarket branch to his harbour. It was authorised in 1857 and work began in 1858, but inexperienced contractors caused delays, so the gestation period was rather prolonged.

The branch, three and a half miles long, began at Granton Junction and struck generally northwards with numerous but fairly modest engineering requirements. A sharp curve from the Haymarket line took the tracks on to an embankment, punctuated by a bridge across the Edinburgh & Glasgow formation and followed by a gentle descent to

the Water of Leith which was crossed on a stone arch. A couple of low spurs from the eastern side of Corstorphine Hill presented a slight barrier but they were easily countered by cuttings spanned respectively by bridges carrying Ravelston Dykes and Queensferry Road. A level section took the tracks to Pilton where a curve to the north east led down to Caroline Park and Granton Harbour. Here there were two sub-branches, one to the main western breakwater and another to the old eastern pier, where a connection with the Edinburgh, Leith & Granton tracks was made. This early double track extension of the Caledonian was substantially constructed, with bridges of rough-hewn stone, and mineral traffic from the west began on 28th August 1861. A passenger service was considered but it never materialised and the Caledonian purchased the Duke of Buccleuch's half share of the line in 1863.

Soon after reaching Granton the Caledonian began planning a route to Leith which promised to provide even more business. The North British branches from Portobello and North Bridge had been established for some time, but they were proving very inconvenient for traffic from the growing industrial areas west of Edinburgh. An extension of two and three quarter miles, from Crewe Junction on the Granton line to Leith western docks, was authorised on 7th July 1862 and it opened for mineral traffic on 1st September 1864. The double-track railway headed roughly eastwards and descended steadily to the shoreline from about 150ft at Crewe Junction, a fair amount of it in shallow cuttings. After crossing Crewe Road North the tracks passed beneath no less than nine bridges on the way to Leith, many of them constructed in later years as housing areas developed. One of the most important overbridges carried Granton Road, and half a mile further on the Caledonian spanned the North British metals between Trinity and Scotland Street. Another significant overbridge carried Lindsay Road, part of the coast highway between Newhaven and Leith. Two half mile spurs opened at the same time as the dock branch, one extending from Pilton West Junction to Pilton East Junction, bypassing Crewe Junction and providing a direct route between Leith and Granton, the other running from Dalry Junction on the main line out of Lothian Road to Coltbridge Junction on the Granton branch. It was largely on an embankment and allowed through working from Lothian Road to the coast.

Over the next twelve years three lines, of very different character, were built. The first opened on 9th July 1869 from Midcalder Junction (on the main line just over eleven miles out of Lothian Road) to Cleland south east of Coatbridge. It crossed the West Lothian and Lanark-

Ex-Caledonian McIntosh '812' class 0-6-0 No.57565 rolled past Dalry Middle Junction with the 1.37pm from Leith North to Edinburgh Princes Street on 19th March 1960. The train is using the 1864 line from Coltbridge Junction whilst the 1876 connection from Haymarket West Junction trails in on the left. Tenements in Downfield Place form the right background and the girder bridge across Dalry Road is immediately in front of the engine. With the construction of the West Approach Road every trace of the railway here has been obliterated.

shire coalfield through West Calder, Addiewell, Fauldhouse and Shotts, thus giving the Caledonian access to an abundant and growing supply of mineral traffic. The line also shortened the distance between Edinburgh and Glasgow considerably and put the company on a much better footing for competing with North British passenger services.

The second line was the delightful Balerno branch which climbed and snaked its way along the narrow wooded Water of Leith Valley a few miles south west of Edinburgh. Its Act was dated 20th June 1870 and passenger services, together with goods services to several mills alongside the track, began on 1st August 1874. The branch began at Balerno Junction, 2½ miles from Princes Street and just south of Slateford viaduct, and immediately crossed the Union Canal and Lanark Road before entering Colinton Dell. A short curved tunnel led to Colinton station (3½ miles from Princes Street) where there was a single platform, a small goods yard and a siding to Scott's oatmeal mill. The general climb continued, punctuated by a few short dips and numerous curves with check rails as far as Juniper Green (4¾ miles) which also had a single platform. A girder bridge carried the rails to the south bank of the river and a descent past Kinleith paper mill siding was followed by a climb to Currie (six miles) where there was a passing loop and two platforms. The line regained the north bank again and the valley became slightly more open, but gradients and curves still abounded. Balerno station (a little over seven miles) had a single platform, next to the overbridge where Lanark Road crossed the railway. It was some way from the village and a short branch to the sepa-

rate goods yard actually served the community somewhat better. The Balerno branch concluded its picturesque course by descending to the main line at Ravelrig Junction (8½ miles) where there were sidings and a platform, although the latter - built in 1884 - was an unadvertised halt and served merely as a convenient operating terminus as far as Water of Leith trains were concerned. Industrial traffic was a feature of the route from completion to closure, but a healthy passenger business developed as well. Numerous villas sprang up in the villages alongside Lanark Road and many resi-

dents used the trains to travel to and from work in Edinburgh. Furthermore, on summer weekends the line became an escape for city dwellers to enjoy a picnic alongside the river or a hike in the Pentland foothills. The little branch had immense character and even enjoyed special treatment when it came to rolling stock. A class of eleven small-wheeled 0-4-4Ts, the 'Balerno Tanks', were built specially for the line, as were a batch of modern four-wheel carriages - long after the type had gone out of general production. Even towards the end there was a good service; in 1935 for example some twenty trains each way made the 25 minute trip to and from Princes Street, while nine workings on summer Sundays catered for pleasure seekers.

Back in Edinburgh itself, the third line of the trio was a very different proposition. It extended for less than three quarters of a mile from Dalry Middle Junction, on the Dalry Junction - Coltbridge Junction spur, to Haymarket West Junction on the main Edinburgh & Glasgow route of the North British. The double track was mainly carried on an embankment and spanned the Slateford - Granton line almost above Granton Junction. Its Act of Parliament was obtained on 30th June 1874 and when the line opened (on 3rd July 1876) Caledonian trains from Edinburgh to the north could exercise running powers over the North British as far as Larbert, before proceeding on their own metals to Stirling, Perth, Dundee and Oban.

The next development involved very little new mileage, yet it was the inauguration of an important passenger service. The Leith and Granton branches were carrying a substantial proportion of the

Caledonian trains from Edinburgh to the north made use of North British metals for part of their journey and this arrangement continued well into BR days. Seen from the brakevan of the South Queensferry goods standing on the Edinburgh & Glasgow line, Standard 2-6-4T No.80125 drifted along the Dalry Middle Junction - Haymarket West Junction spur with the 11.40am from Princes Street to Stirling, on 26th December 1962. One arm of the Southside Suburban line comes in on the extreme right whilst the other is in front of the factories in the distance. Westfield Road, which serves this industrial area, was spanned by girder bridges carrying the various tracks.

Very smartly turned out Standard class 5 4-6-0s Nos. 73060 and 73076 from Polmadie shed eased along the line between Slateford and Coltbridge Junction with the 12.40pm dining car excursion from Glasgow Central to Murrayfield for the Scotland -v- England Rugby International on 19th March 1960. These trains originated in Caledonian days when they were composed of Pullman cars. The Dalry Middle Junction - Haymarket West Junction tracks of 1876 cross the view from left to right, the original 1853 branch from Slateford to Haymarket passing under the brick arch on the left. Granton Junction, where the 1861 line to Granton (being used by the train) diverged, lies just beyond the overbridge.

The inauguration of passenger services on the Leith branch included new stations at Craigleith, Granton Road and Newhaven. All three were built next to existing masonry overbridges and were of similar construction. Robust side platforms reached by wooden stairways contrasted with the rather dull timber buildings carried on lattice girders, adjacent to the road bridges but separate from them. Granton Road was typical. Neither the woodwork nor slate roof displayed special qualities and the chimneys were decidedly plain. On the far side an open footbridge linking the stairways was attached to the outside of the building. Little timber sheds provided shelter on the platforms. In this view Standard tram No.37 reversed at Granton Road on 16th November 1956. The station was served by routes 23 and 27 from Morningside and Firrhill respectively, although only the former was operating by this time. Granton Road station building was demolished in 1985 but the identical structure at Newhaven is still used, by a joinery firm.

burgeoning dock traffic but the demand for suburban passenger services to Edinburgh was also growing. During 1878 separate tracks were laid from Newhaven to a new terminus in Lindsay Road on the western edge of Leith. This was a fairly simple affair with a single island platform partly sheltered by a rudimentary train shed. Four intermediate stations were also built - at Craighall Road in Newhaven; next to Granton Road; south of Queensferry Road in Craigleith and at Roseburn Terrace east of Murrayfield. Another was added at Dalry Road near the main line during 1900. Passenger services from Princes Street to Leith commenced on 1st August 1879 with twelve trains each way on weekdays,

largely formed of four-wheel coaches hauled by elderly 0-4-4 tanks or 0-4-2 tender locos. By the 1930s there were almost forty services in each direction - reflecting the importance of the line for local journeys - and bogie vehicles with sturdy 0-4-4Ts were the norm. A passenger service to Granton was envisaged at first, though it failed to materialise; however, at the turn of the century a huge gasworks was built in open country west of the harbour and workmen's trains began to serve a private station on the edge of the site from 1st November 1902. These were advertised as far as Craigleith but did not appear in the timetable thence to Granton, despite being used by some local residents.

During the final decade of the 19th century there was a modest addition to the Caledonian system on the west side of Edinburgh and it proved fairly successful, although usually far less busy than the Leith line. The branch from Craigleith to Cramond Brig was authorised on 25th July 1890 and after a somewhat leisurely construction period it opened to passenger and goods traffic on 1st March 1894. From about 150ft above sea level the double track headed north west past Drylaw to a summit of just over 200ft at Davidson's Mains. It then veered south west and descended to 150ft again about half a mile from Cramond Bridge where Queensferry Road crosses the River Almond. The gentle climb and slightly indirect course were necessitated by a prominent spur from Corstorphine Hill. In addition to the terminus, there was an intermediate station at Davidson's Mains near the junction of Cramond Road, Quality Street and Main Street, a mile and a half from Craigleith. This was originally called Barnton Gate but was renamed Davidson's Mains on 1st April 1903 when the terminus at Cramond Brig became Barnton. The pleasant pastures between Corstorphine Hill and the River Almond were already becoming a wealthy residential area when the line opened and the Caledonian immediately planned an extension south westwards to Lennie Park then eastwards through North Gyle and Corstorphine back to Dalry Road. This suburban circle failed to materialise but the worthies of Barnton nevertheless enjoyed a service of 24 trains a day to and from Princes Street in Edwardian times. In addition there were five or more extras on Saturday and even a Sunday service in summer to cater for trippers to Cramond on the Firth of Forth. By 1930 the service had decreased slightly to twenty trains each way, the journey from Princes Street to Barnton taking sixteen minutes, but there were still six return workings on Sunday afternoon and evening for excursionists. Unfortunately the growth of car ownership in this affluent area was already beginning to erode receipts by this time.

Leith North terminus; originally simply Leith, then North Leith from August 1903 to April 1952, it exuded simplicity despite its fairly intensive service. There were no run-round loops and until the advent of diesel multiple units, trains had to reverse out of the station after arrival, the engine then running round its stock before backing into the station again. The stubby overall roof was largely built of timber and had one open side supported by columns and another formed of a brick wall bordering Lindsay Road. Beyond a tiny concourse the train shed was integrated with a rather bleak entrance building in brown brick with white relief around doors and windows. It was a poor show compared with the lovely Caledonian architecture which emerged a decade or so later. On 21st May 1955 McIntosh 0-6-0 No.57559 waited at Leith North with the 12.05pm to Edinburgh Princes Street as a tram headed east along Lindsay Road. Thirty years after closure, part of the island platform survived and the building was being used by a firm hiring marquees. Some fine old warehouses survived near the junction of Commercial Street and North Junction Street in 1994 but the area was dominated by two horrific 1960s concrete tower blocks, awaiting demolition.

In an attempt to counter road and tramway competition, the LMS opened a couple of new stations in the 1930s, both of them rather basic affairs. The Leith branch gained East Pilton (next to Pilton Road overbridge) on 1st December 1934; it served a number of engineering factories and consisted of side platforms reached by steps, and the simplest type of wooden buildings. House O'Hill Halt near Corbiehill Avenue on the Barnton branch came on 1st February 1937 and was equally austere. From then on the picture was one of decline and eventually wholesale closure. The Granton Gasworks service faded away during the wartime gloom of 1942, followed by the end of the Balerno branch passenger trains on 1st November 1943. Barnton passenger services ceased on 7th May 1951 and the ter-

minus goods yard closed on the same day. Then there was a lull before the onslaught, the only casualties over the next eleven years being goods facilities at Juniper Green (11th August 1958) and Craigleith and Davidson's Mains, on 1st June 1960. A serious blow to the Edinburgh suburban network was the loss of Princes Street - Leith North passenger trains on 30th August 1962, when they were still carrying an average of two thousand passengers each weekday. So far, the only sizeable length of actual track to have disappeared was the Barnton branch, but that was about to change.

Balerno to Ravelrig Junction closed completed on 9th September 1963, with Dalry Junction - Coltbridge Junction and Dalry Middle Junction - Haymarket West Junction succumbing on 9th March 1964. Five days earlier, passenger trains from Stirling and beyond had been diverted from Princes Street to Waverley. At last there was a reopening, or at least a reinstatement, when the Duff Street connection was put in at Haymarket and passenger trains began to run through from Slateford on 7th September 1964 - a prelude, of course, to the much more serious closure of Princes Street itself. Murrayfield goods, merely an unstaffed public siding since the end of passenger services, finished on 21st June 1965. Traffic from Crewe Junction to Granton Gasworks ended on 2nd August 1965, Granton Junction to North Leith perished on 4th September 1967 and the rest of the Balerno branch went on 4th December 1967. Finally, goods facilities at Granton High and North Leith were withdrawn on 5th February and 5th August 1968 respectively, both of them latterly served by connections from the former North British system. By this time the Caledonian network in Edinburgh had been virtually obliterated. A crumb of comfort has been the conversion of several sections into walkways, notably the Balerno and Leith branches.

TOO MUCH TOO LATE

One section of Caledonian line in Edinburgh has yet to be described. It stands apart from the others as part of a grandiose plan for a circular route on the north side involving all manner of expensive engineering works including large girder bridges, long viaducts, deep tunnels and 'cut and cover' excavations through the heart of the city. Almost all the land to be occupied by the projected railway was already built over and more than a dozen station sites were suggested at one time or another, some of them below ground. Although similar in scope to the company's ambitious suburban system on the north side of Glasgow, this particular scheme was never completed. It did provide Leith Docks with yet another line, which was costly enough, but the underground section faltered and its value to

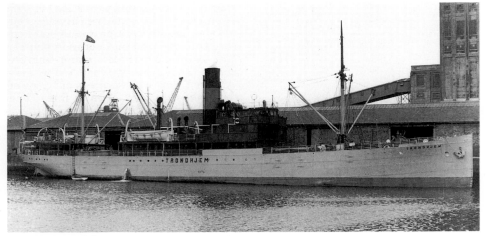

A fine old Danish cargo steamer TRONDHJEM, probably dating from the early 1900s, was berthed at Albert Dock in Leith on 29th August 1955. It had the traditional straight prow and counter stern. Traffic at the port mainly comprised imported esparto grass for paper making, pit props and other timber, and Danish bacon and dairy produce. Exports included coal, engineering products and various manufactured goods. Leith, unlike Glasgow and Greenock on the west coast, remains relatively busy with shipping traffic in the 1990s.

Granton Gasworks station, built by the Edinburgh and Leith Gas Commissioners, was a remarkable place for a private industrial terminus. It had an island platform, the eastern face of which extended beneath a more than adequate building clearly reflecting the municipal magnificence of late Victorian and Edwardian years. The structure consisted of a two storey red brick block with a hipped slate roof, but plenty of detailed decoration was incorporated. Vaguely classical pilasters (attached columns) in white brick adorned the walls and the ample upper floor waiting room had large Tudor windows with stone surrounds. Ground floor rooms had round-headed windows whilst an open arcade on the platform side let the Firth of Forth breezes in. A lattice footbridge across the gasworks sidings was the main access and homegoing workers were greeted by a fine Jacobean dormer with a ball finial, weathervane and clock. On 21st May 1955 J88 0-6-0T No.68320 had brought loaded coal wagons into the complex and Scottish Gas Board No.7 in the background was about to shunt them.

the local transport scene will never be known. Had it materialised, the capital may well have gained a durable suburban network served today by electric trains!

The 'Leith New Lines' were inspired by the Edinburgh Dock at Leith, which was completed in 1881 and occupied 54 acres of reclaimed land, the cost being shared by the Caledonian and North British. An eastwards extension to Seafield from the existing Leith branch was announced at the end of 1889 and this was to have a passenger terminus at Salamander Street near the North British South Leith station. A line back to Princes Street

would have started at a triangular junction near Lochend followed by embankments and viaducts across Hillside, a tunnel below Calton Hill as far as St. James Square and 'cut and cover' beneath George Street. From there the tracks were to veer south to a junction with the main line just outside Princes Street. A short underground branch would have served a terminus at Waverley Market, next to the rival North British premises. Leith councillors were enthusiastic and wanted half a dozen local stations, but Edinburgh Corporation was aghast at the prospect of city streets being torn up and strongly objected to the proposals. As a result the Act of 4th July 1890 sanctioned only the Newhaven to Seafield section. Undaunted, the Caledonian revived its plans to include a spacious station under St. James Square instead of the Waverley Market spur and included connections to the North British at Easter Road and Haymarket. The Easter Road spur, but precious little else, was allowed by the Edinburgh & Leith Junction Act of 3rd July 1891, thus effectively killing off the scheme. Work began on the dock line during 1899 after frustrating attempts to buy land between Bonnington and Leith Walk forced a deviation Act in 1894. The line opened on 1st August 1903 but the almost completed passenger stations at Newhaven, Ferry Road and Leith Walk never opened and the track was singled in 1917. A steady flow of goods traffic - together with one or two special passenger trains - used the line over the years, but through workings finished with the closure of Newhaven Junction to Leith Walk on 4th January 1966. Leith Walk West goods depot and the line to Leith closed on 6th May 1968, although Leith East yard (South Leith until April 1952) lasted until 31st December 1973.

The character of the line can be judged from notes taken by W.A.C. Smith during a brake van trip aboard the 2.20pm freight working from Slateford yard to Leith East on Boxing Day 1961. The co-author and companion had acquired the necessary permit but as railway staff they were excused payment of the mandatory first class (!) fare. They boarded the train in one of the down sidings where the St. Margarets steam crane was unloading girders for the Forth Road Bridge, then under construction, and D49 4-4-0 No.62712 MORAYSHIRE (later to be preserved) was derelict after a spell as a stationary boiler at the nearby railway laundry. Eventually McIntosh 0-6-0 No.57565 arrived from Dalry Road shed and the train left at 3.08pm. The engine was running tender first and its cab storm sheet provided little protection for the footplate crew in the heavy snowfall...

'At Newhaven Junction we got the single line staff and swung away from the Leith passenger lines and goods loops on to the Leith New Lines past a pair of brick

Granton was once a busy fishing port with a fleet of ocean-going vessels, and much of the catch was despatched by rail. Seen in 1952, GN.37 DRUMSHEUGH typified the classic steam trawler with its straight bow, counter stern and elegant sheer to the deckline. A wealth of detail included huge winches, steaming and riding lights on the raked foremast, big ventilator cowls and a galley chimney in best hillbilly tradition. Otter boards for keeping the net open were stored forward of the lifeboat and a curved 'turtle' deck was provided at the prow for rapid dispersal of sea water in rough weather.

faced platforms in the junction fork, then through Victoria Park where the site of a spur which would have formed a triangle with the Leith North Line was evident. Having curved sharply down through the platforms of never completed Ferry Road station and past the disused Chancelot Mills siding, the train climbed across a plate girder bridge above the three-way Bonnington East Junction (on the Leith Citadel branch) beside the Water of Leith. It then crossed a viaduct and a bowstring girder bridge where our engine uncoupled and went down into Rosebank goods depot, but there was no traffic on offer. Setting off again, at a brisk pace, we crossed a massive girder bridge over Pilrig Street where the earthworks of a temporary halt (provided for a military review held in 1908) were visible. After the tenements of Bonnington Road, a siding dropped away on the right into the quite extensive Leith Walk West goods yard, situated not much more than a stone's throw from Leith Central diesel depot. On a sandstone viaduct behind a cinema were lengthy platforms with facing but no decking, intended for Leith Walk passenger station. Two more bridges and a climb along an embankment past a mill siding and a timber yard followed, then we went down a sharp curve in a cutting and crossed the Leith Central branch near

Besides providing the Caledonian with a direct route between Edinburgh and Glasgow, the Shotts line was used by certain longer distance trains, notably holiday traffic. With pristine B1 4-6-0 No.61261 in charge, the summer Saturdays 9.20am from Heads of Ayr to Edinburgh Princes Street passed West Calder on 25th May 1963. Note the Caledonian route indicator over the buffer beam - an odd sight on an ex-LNER engine! A huge shale oil bing is prominent in the background, typifying the industrial nature of these tracks through the coalfield. In marked contrast the station buildings at West Calder were very attractive single storey structures with huge low-pitched roofs and prominent eaves, dominated by projecting timbers.

Inevitably, the trams had an adverse effect on passenger loadings at Colinton, once they had been extended from Craiglockhart in 1926. Routes 9 (from Granton Square) and 10 (from Bernard Street) terminated at Bridge Street near the centre of the village and were far more convenient than the station down in its cutting. Trams Nos.167, 189 and 91 waited at Colinton terminus on 10th April 1955 shortly before Edinburgh Corporation buses replaced them.

Easter Road Park football platform. Continuing down a long cutting, we emerged at the site of sidings above the Firth of Forth at Seafield Junction. A high embankment with sandstone retaining walls followed, and, after skirting Claremont Park, we came to a halt outside Leith East goods at 3.39pm, with darkness already falling. The loco was uncoupled, a few vans were run into a siding, and the brake van was put alongside the loading bank which was occupied by wagons of scrap. The yard handled a lot of traffic for private sidings and was well filled with vans and tank wagons as well as more steelwork for the Forth Road Bridge. We retired with the crew to the shunter's bothy for a cup of tea, and then after much shunting the loco picked up seven vans of biscuits from Crawford's siding. At about 5.40pm we charged back up to Seafield Junction ground frame and in blizzard conditions the engine propelled the train across the bridge spanning Seafield Road and deposited the vans in a siding above South Leith yard, ready to be worked to Hardengreen where they were to join a class C freight ...'

The travellers then thumbed a lift aboard Birmingham - Sulzer Type 2 No.D5357 on the 6.40pm class H freight to Cadder Yard and the driver obligingly slowed to walking pace at Morningside Road to let them alight.

This view of Juniper Green station on 12th May 1956 typifies what was one of the most attractive suburban routes in the country, let alone Edinburgh. The Water of Leith is off to the right and Lanark Road, together with the village itself, is masked by trees on the left. A solitary coal wagon occupies the goods yard. All four original stations on the line were provided with little timber buildings featuring a gently sloping roof extending well beyond the walls to form a modest canopy. Doors and windows were quite plain, but the canopy valance was very decorative and a clock was provided on the platform side. The branch gained an extra station when Hailes Platform near Colinton opened on 16th November 1908, to serve a nearby golf course.

Another reflection of the sharp curves on the Balerno branch was the use of 0-4-2 tender locos for goods traffic well into LMS days. No.17013, built for the Caledonian by Dubs & Co. in 1881, rested at Dalry Road shed - probably around 1930 - between trips along the Water of Leith Valley, shunting yards and mill sidings. The engine was withdrawn for scrapping in 1931. One of the ex-Caledonian 30 ton bogie mineral wagons can be seen at the coaling stage. Photograph J.J. Cunningham.

4 in class

-4-4 well tank trailing bogies o/side

inders. Coupled wheels 4'8" diam.

inders 17x22 1873-4 by Neilson & Co

8,169 Leith 170 on Balerno 167 spare

broken up 1899

. 111 0-4-4T by JF McIntosh

Rollox 1899 17x24 4'6" wheels.

tidrawn 1930

-uyers Archive Special Advertising

Photography 2 www. IUERZ ARCHIVE.COM

Also p55 top right

1200 film 12 fr.

Spectra Image 990 10 fr.

Seafield engine shed epitomised the folly of the Caledonian's Leith New Lines. It opened in 1902 and consisted of a simple but solid two road brick building, a coaling stage and several stabling tracks. It soon proved superfluous and was leased to the North British during World War I! A period of disuse followed until the LNER decided to outstation freight engines there in order to relieve congestion at St. Margarets during World War II, and this role continued until closure in October 1962. On 7th November 1959 J35 0-6-0 No.64532, J36 0-6-0 No.65224 MONS and J38 0-6-0 No.65918 had retired to Seafield. Also present on this Saturday afternoon were another three J35s and four J37s. In the adjoining South Leith yard, at a filled-in turntable pit marking the site of the one-time North British South Leith shed, were an N15 0-6-2T and several diesel shunters. Noted at Seafield on 25th August 1962 some two months before closure, were a J36, three J37s and two J38s. A V2, three V3s and a pair of N15s were dumped awaiting scrapping.

One of several options for the Caledonian's circular suburban route involved excavating Princes Street. A similar line under Argyle Street in Glasgow was successfully completed, but howls of outrage ensured that this one had little chance of coming to fruition. On 3rd September 1955 tram No.202 headed west along Princes Street towards Fairmilehead. The spiky spire of the Scott Monument is on the right, Calton Hill's distinctive skyline closes the view, and the tower of the North British Hotel stands sentinel over the traffic. If Waverley Market underground terminus had materialised it would have been accessible from Princes Street, immediately this side of the hotel.

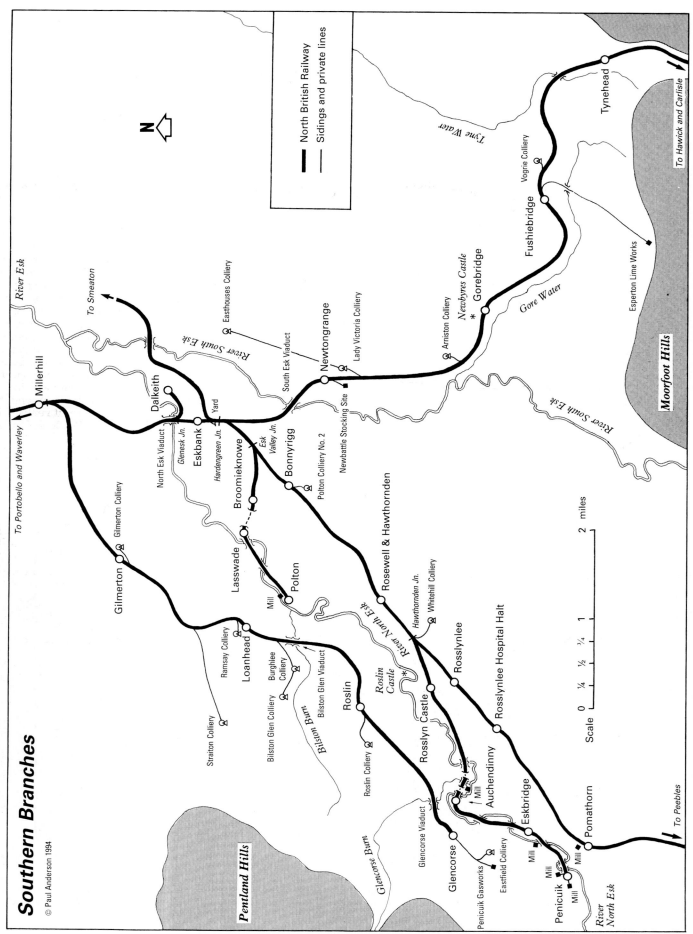

Southern Branches

© Paul Anderson 1994

N

North British Railway

Sidings and private lines

River Esk

To Smeaton

Millerhill

To Portobello and Waverley

Dalkeith

Yard

Eskbank

Glenesk Jn.

North Esk Viaduct

Hardengreen Jn.

Broomieknowe

Gilmerton Colliery

Gilmerton

Bonnyrigg

Esk Valley Jn.

River South Esk

Easthouses Colliery

South Esk Viaduct

Newtongrange

Newbattle Stocking Site

Polton Colliery No. 2

Lady Victoria Colliery

Arniston Colliery

Newbyres Castle

* Gorebridge

Fushiebridge

Gore Water

Vogrie Colliery

Tynehead

Tyne Water

To Hawick and Carlisle

Esperton Lime Works

Moorfoot Hills

River South Esk

Rosewell & Hawthornden

Hawthornden Jn.

Whitehill Colliery

Lasswade

Polton

Mill

River North Esk

Ramsay Colliery

Loanhead

Burghlee Colliery

Straiton Colliery

Bilston Glen Colliery

Bilston Glen Viaduct

Bilston Burn

Roslin

Roslin Colliery

Roslin Castle
*

Rosslyn Castle

Rosslynlee

Rosslynlee Hospital Halt

Auchendinny

Mill

Eskbridge

Pomathorn

To Peebles

Glencorse Burn

Glencorse Viaduct

Glencorse

Penicuik Gasworks

Eastfield Colliery

Mill

Mill

Penicuik

Mill

Mill

River North Esk

Pentland Hills

Scale

0   ¼   ½   ¾   1   2 miles

62

Chapter Four

Southern Branches

As noted earlier, the pioneering Edinburgh & Dalkeith Railway and its feeder waggonways had to build substantial viaducts where they encountered the River North Esk and River South Esk respectively in the vicinity of Dalkeith. Between 1845 and 1877 no less than five separate lines springing from the former horse operated system were pushed south through this difficult terrain. The earliest was the Edinburgh & Hawick which eventually became part of the famous Waverley route. A long viaduct across the South Esk near Newbattle was required before the tracks swung away eastwards to tackle the wild slopes and deep valleys of the Moorfoot Hills, but the river itself presented no further problems to this or subsequent railways. The North Esk was a very different matter. South west of Dalkeith it gouged a deep wooded valley through the broad tableland below the Pentland Hills and this very attractive countryside was thoroughly explored by

branches of various lengths. All of them were privately promoted and had their own distinctive characteristics, yet in effect they were part of the North British network from the outset and were soon absorbed by the larger company. The Peebles Railway serving the delightful Tweedside town some twenty miles south of Edinburgh was the first to open, in 1855. It kept to the airy ground south east of the valley in order to avoid major engineering works, but also missed most existing settlements, apart from Bonnyrigg. Before long nearby Lasswade, Loanhead, Polton, Roslin, Auchendinny and Penicuik also wanted their own railways to Edinburgh and set about promoting them. The North British actively supported the new lines from their conception because of known local coal reserves, the important paper mills in the valleys and the prospect of residential traffic to the city. Somewhat remarkably, the Esk Valley Railway, Penicuik Railway and Edinburgh, Loanhead & Roslin Railway, along with

the Peebles Railway, provided no less than fifteen stations in less then twelve square miles of the rural North Esk valley.

HAWICK AND PEEBLES

One of the most lamentable railway closures in Britain was the Waverley route from Edinburgh to Carlisle in 1969. Its demise was sanctioned by Transport Minister Barbara Castle six years after the Beeching Report and even after the 1968 Transport Act had come into force, intended to stem the haemorrhage of marginal and uneconomic passenger services. The line did not duplicate other routes and over the last 25 years the Border communities of Galashiels, Melrose, St. Boswells and Hawick have stagnated. However, the railway across the Southern Uplands was certainly not regarded as an asset in its early years and indeed the North British considered closing it a few years after completion. It realised its full potential when the Settle & Carlisle

The Marquis of Lothian's waggonway from Dalhousie Mains to Arniston crossed the River South Esk by a spectacular 334 yard viaduct consisting of timber decking on cast iron gothic arches supported by slender sandstone piers. When the Edinburgh & Hawick was constructed the structure was widened to take double track and rebuilt with conventional brick and stone arches. B1 4-6-0 No.61341 crossed Newbattle viaduct with the 5.11pm from Edinburgh Waverley to Galashiels on 24th May 1962.

With Newtongrange station in the distance, Birmingham/Sulzer Type 2 No.D5308 hurried past Lady Victoria Pit signal box and the large colliery itself with the 5.57pm Edinburgh Waverley to Carlisle on 11th May 1963. Lady Victoria mine and Newbattle opencast site on the left still had a fascinating selection of NCB Lothians Area shunting engines in the late 1960s. These included Grant Ritchie and Andrew Barclay 0-4-2STs and a couple of 0-4-0STs thought to have been built by the Newbattle United Colliery Company.

opened in 1876 and through expresses to West Yorkshire, the East Midlands and London St. Pancras were inaugurated in conjunction with the Midland Railway.

The Waverley route had its origins in the Edinburgh & Hawick Railway which was authorised on 31st July 1845, having been promoted by an independent company which relinquished its powers to the North British a few days before the Act was passed. Authority for an extension to Carlisle was also sought but this was thrown out by parliament at an early stage. The Hawick branch opened as far as Gorebridge on 14th July 1847 - just thirteen months after the main line to Berwick - and reached its destination on 1st November 1849. From Hawick Junction (later Portobello East Junction) the tracks veered south from the coast route and joined the former Edinburgh & Dalkeith east of Niddrie. The old formation through Millerhill, Sheriffhall and Hardengreen to Dalhousie was completely rebuilt to take heavier trains, as was the Marquis of Lothian's waggonway to Arniston. This work involved reconstructing viaducts across the North and South Esk at Eskbank and Newbattle respectively. Beyond Arniston new construction took the line eastwards past Newbyres Castle and into a cutting

through Gorebridge. A relentless eight mile climb at 1 in 70 had begun and during the ascent the track twisted and carved its way up the Gore Water valley past Fushiebridge to Tynehead and the wild slopes of the Moorfoot Hills. From

Falahill summit, nearly 900ft above the Firth of Forth, the Edinburgh & Hawick took advantage of the deep Gala Water valley to reach the Border textile towns.

Eight Hawthorn 2-4-0s were built for the line and they worked the meagre pas-

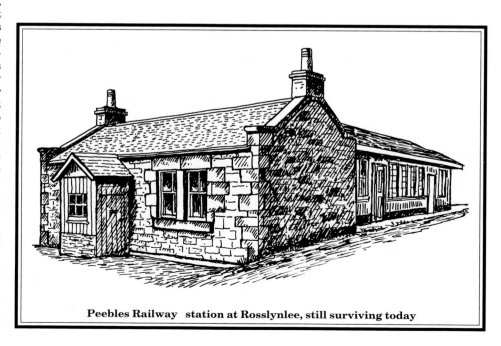

Peebles Railway station at Rosslynlee, still surviving today

National Coal Board Lothians Area No.6, an Andrew Barclay 0-4-2ST dating from 1910, shunted Lady Victoria Colliery in bright sunshine on 18th May 1967.

senger service which in 1849 consisted of three departures from Edinburgh, at 8.15am, 10.45am and 4.30pm. The branch had cost a lot of money and many shareholders considered that the North British had overstretched itself, some even suggesting closure of the line. Trains continued to run, however, and the traffic in

high quality Tweed cloth increased. With the company's finances on a firmer footing, an extension to Carlisle in the form of the Border Union Railway was sanctioned on 21st July 1859 and the Waverley route opened throughout on 1st June 1862 after fierce counter proposals from the Caledonian. Despite the initial concern

about the viability of the route it soon developed into a vital link to Edinburgh and England for the mill towns and farming communities of Selkirkshire and Roxburghshire. Livestock was carried in abundance, tourists flocked to see 'Scott country', rugby specials headed for internationals at Murrayfield and residents were reassured by the sound of the 'Night Midland' heading south. The Edinburgh & Dalkeith directors could hardly have imagined this amount of activity on their modest line to the Lothian coalfield.

During the 19th century Peebles developed as a woollen manufacturing centre and popular spa resort, the latter helped by its picturesque location where Eddleston Water met the River Tweed amid the beautiful folds of the Moorfoot Hills. In 1841 it was the unlikely headquarters of the proposed National Railway of Scotland which intended to build a line from Lancaster to Edinburgh and Glasgow through the town. Perhaps inevitably this project faded into oblivion and when the Edinburgh & Hawick wound its way along Gala Water twelve miles away beyond bleak Leithen Hopes and Deaf Heights in 1849, the residents of Peebles were understandably upset. On a less grandiose level than the National Railway, local interests promoted the Peebles Railway which received its Act

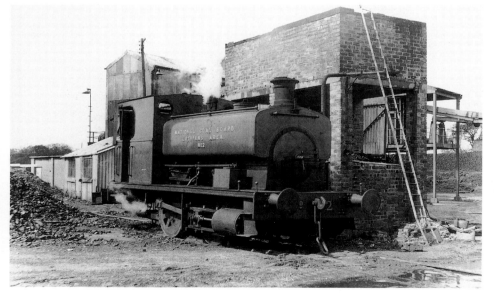

NCB Lothians Area No.2, a Grant Ritchie 0-4-0ST dating from 1879 but subsequently rebuilt, rested alongside the water tower at Newbattle Coal Stocking Site, 18th May 1967.

At Arniston Engine, near the terminus of the Marquis of Lothian's waggonway, the Hawick line became pleasantly rural, with the wooded slopes of the South Esk and Gore Water valleys slipping away to the west. Standard 2-6-4T No.80055 headed into the sweeping curve south of Lady Victoria pit in charge of the 5.11pm from Edinburgh Waverley to Gorebridge on 11th May 1963. The modest girder bridge carried a driveway to Kirkhill Hotel down by the South Esk; the stone arch beyond it was on the minor road from Carrington to Arniston.

on 8th July 1853 and opened less then two years later on 4th July 1855. The single track branch, nearly nineteen miles, left the Hawick line at Hardengreen Junction just south of Eskbank about 200ft above sea level and climbed steadily along the eastern shoulder of the North Esk valley at up to 1 in 53, reaching 300ft at Bonnyrigg (a mile from the junction) 500ft at Rosewell (two and three quarter miles), 600ft at Rosslynlee (four and a quarter miles) and 750ft at Pomathorn, two and a half miles further on than that. By this time a fine panorama of the Pentland Hills had opened up with the wooded gorge of the North Esk providing a delightful foreground. The line then headed across open country to Leadburn, nearly 950ft above sea level, before dropping down the lovely Eddelston Water valley to Peebles, just above the 500ft contour.

Although the line was built as cheaply as possible with level crossings instead of road bridges, it was extremely well managed and was profitable from the outset. The directors and shareholders were local people who cared passionately about their railway and although happily taking advice from the North British, were determined to have full control over day to day operations. After a disappointing approach to an outside contractor, the Peebles Railway purchased two Neilson

Almost hidden from sight, midway along a mile and a quarter cutting through the watershed between Tyne Water and Cakemuir Burn, was Tynehead station. When this northwards looking view was taken on 11th May 1963 the station had just one train each way a day, and none at all on Saturday and Sunday. This meagre service was hardly surprising considering the remoteness of the place. With bleak Fala Moor immediately to the east and the Moorfoot Hills rising towards the south west, the only settlements were a scattering of farmsteads together with the villages of Pathhead and Fala, several miles away to the north. The little hamlet of Tynehead was next to the line and acquired a rather pleasant single storey station house when the Hawick branch was built. Nearby Fushiebridge station - which also stood amid lightly populated countryside - at least had some industrial activity, in the form of a privately owned branch to Esperston Lime Works, operated by a Manning Wardle 0-6-0ST. The works also had a narrow gauge system.

The first station on the Peebles Railway was Bonnyrigg, about quarter of a mile from the centre of this large workaday village which straddles the Dalkeith to Leadburn road. Although fairly conveniently located, it was actually renamed Bonnyrigg Road between December 1866 and August 1868, to distinguish it from nearby Bonnyrigg station on the Polton line. In this view the original building, a little grey stone structure, was hidden by later accretions. A Gloucester diesel multiple unit forming the 3.54pm from Edinburgh Waverley to Rosewell & Hawthornden drew into Bonnyrigg on 2nd September 1962, a week before the service was withdrawn. New houses now occupy the trackbed beyond the level crossing, but in 1994 the platforms survived and had been attractively landscaped. The original Peebles Railway building lingered on in a derelict state and the goods shed had been turned into a workshop.

2-4-0s and a pair of Hawthorn 0-4-2s to haul its passenger and goods trains respectively. The former comprised three services each way between Peebles and Edinburgh taking about two hours, with the local company's engines exchanged for North British motive power at Eskbank. This arrangement lasted for almost six

years, until the North British began working the line on 1st February 1861. The Peebles Railway was leased to the larger company from 11th July 1861 and was absorbed by it on 1st August 1876. Meanwhile an extension to Galashiels had been opened during 1866 and effectively provided a loop off the Waverley route. Throughout its 107 year life the railway to Peebles was predominantly a pedestrian local line, although in Edwardian years the 'Peebles-shire Express' leaving the Border town just before 9.00am and returning in late afternoon, proved to be one of the most prestigious Edinburgh residential services.

Waverley route expresses were always in the hands of the best North British locomotives including the handsome Atlantics in later pre-grouping years. Class D49 4-4-0s partly displaced North British 'Glen' and 'Scott' 4-4-0s in LNER days whilst Gresley A3s were introduced on principal services in the 1930s. The Pacifics had a long reign until main line diesels took over for the last decade or so. For many years Peebles trains were hauled by 'Scott' 4-4-0s but B1 4-6-0s appeared briefly in the 1950s and Gloucester diesel railcars had a monopoly from 1958. Remote Fushiebridge, on the Waverley route east of Gorebridge, closed to passengers on 4th October 1943 although it remained open for goods traffic until 1st January 1959. The following 3rd August saw the end of the yard at

On 16th July 1962 a Gloucester railcar departed from Rosewell & Hawthornden with the 2.37pm service to Edinburgh Waverley. This station had been called plain Hawthornden until 9th July 1928. Hawthornden itself was a tiny farming hamlet and has never expanded. Rosewell, on the other hand, is a remarkable place. From modest rural origins it became a colliery village pure and simple, with row upon row of single storey miners' cottages which remain in original condition to this day. The fairly substantial station buildings have gone but the platforms remain amid a wilderness of gorse bushes, and the trackbed is a pleasant footpath offering views of the distant Pentland Hills. The Peebles Railway was doubled between Hardengreen Junction and Hawthornden Junction to accommodate extra traffic from the Penicuik line and with all Galashiels and Penicuik trains calling, Rosewell & Hawthornden had a reasonable service during LNER and early BR days. In May 1930 there were eleven weekday workings from Waverley and four more on Saturdays, including departures at 11.00pm and 11.18pm from the city. By May 1948 this was down to seven on weekdays plus two on Saturdays, taking between 23 and 27 minutes.

Rosslynlee station was in a remote spot on a country lane running past Gourlaw and Rosslynlee farms. It was originally called Roslin, although the village was almost two miles away along steep twisting roads and a horse conveyance provided connections with the trains. The North British forced a change of name on 2nd September 1872 when a station opened on the Penicuik line slightly nearer Roslin. From 1st January 1917 to 2nd July 1919 Rosslynlee was closed completely and it became an unstaffed halt on 3rd August 1959. Its isolation was further emphasised by the lack of passengers for the 12.21pm from Edinburgh Waverley to Galashiels via Peebles on 1st November 1961. In 1994 the station was virtually in original condition and handsomely repaid a visit. The strange little Peebles Railway building in grey stone faced the road, and its gable end walls were extended above the roof line to form a parapet with small shoulders. It had simple square windows, yet the entrance consisted of a more than adequate porch with its own pyramidal slate roof. A timber panelled structure, of North British origin, extended along the platform and incorporated waiting rooms.

Rosslynlee on the Peebles line. Passenger trains from Edinburgh to Galashiels via Peebles ended on 5th February 1962 although a local service from Waverley to Rosewell & Hawthornden was maintained until 10th September 1962. Freight traffic ceased to use the respective stretches of track at the same time as passenger services, but Bonnyrigg yard was served by a stub from Hardengreen Junction until 25th January 1965. Meanwhile the Waverley route was living on borrowed time, Gorebridge and Tynehead becoming unstaffed halts on 27th March 1967, having lost goods facilities on 28th December 1964. The withdrawal of passenger trains between Edinburgh Waverley, Hawick and Carlisle was effective from 6th January 1969.

POLTON, PENICUIK AND GLENCORSE

Encouraged by the early success of the Peebles line, there was a flurry of railway promotion in and around the North Esk valley over the following couple of decades. Polton, almost hidden in the gorge but the site of several mills, was the first place to show interest. Discussions began in January 1861 and the Esk Valley Railway received its Act on 21st July 1863. Construction work started in September 1864 and trains began running

on 15th April 1867, the prolonged gestation period for a line just over two miles long being partly the result of demanding engineering requirements but largely because of opposition from the Caledonian, which wished to claim the territory for itself. From Esk Valley Junction on the Peebles line the rails climbed steadily westwards through a substantial cutting, spanned by the Dalkeith - Leadburn road. Broomieknowe station (not much more than half a mile from the junction) was on the northern edge of Bonnyrigg; indeed until 1st August 1868 the nameboards carried that name. Shortly afterwards the branch descended through a 430 yard tunnel and began its brief but difficult encounter with the North Esk valley. Lasswade station (at a mile) was in an awkward and rather remote spot immediately beyond the tunnel and opened on 12th October 1868, after the local company bowed to North British pressure to provide it. A high six-arch stone viaduct then curved gracefully across the valley and the rails dropped sharply down the hillside before regaining the south bank by a much lower two-span girder bridge across the river. The cramped terminus at Polton followed after about half a mile, the only other access to this little mill village being precipitous minor roads. Having leased and worked it from the outset, the North British absorbed the Esk Valley Railway on 13th July 1871.

Just over a year earlier one of the most remarkable and scenic branches in the Edinburgh area was sanctioned, the four and a quarter miles of the Penicuik Railway exploring the North Esk valley intimately and crossing the river no less than seven times in just two and a half miles. Furthermore, it was heavily engineered virtually throughout its length and as most of it is now a footpath this work can still be examined in detail. Penicuik is an ancient settlement and served as a

After a monotonous diet of Gloucester diesel multiple units for several years, the Peebles line went out in fine style with a steam special. The Stephenson Locomotive Society 'Farewell to Peebles' railtour, hauled by J37 0-6-0 No.64587, paused at Rosslynlee Hospital Halt on 3rd February 1962. This isolated station surrounded by plantations on the southern slopes of the North Esk valley, was basic to say the least. It opened as late as 11th December 1958 and was served by all trains.

The 12.21pm from Edinburgh Waverley to Galashiels via Peebles, a Gloucester railcar again, drew into Pomathorn on 20th January 1962. Here the Peebles Railway building had conventional gable ends and the North British addition in brick and timber was separate. The station was called Penicuik until 2nd September 1872 when that town acquired its own terminus, and became an unstaffed halt on 1st November 1946. Although much altered, the original stone structure survived as a house in 1994 and presented an interesting contrast to the huge and largely derelict red brick mill nearby. The Pentland summits of West Kip, Scald Law and Carnethy Hill provided a noble backdrop. The severe gradients on the Peebles line called for a special instruction to staff and in LNER days this read 'Under no circumstances whatever must wagons be shunted at any station or siding between Hardengreen Junction and Leadburn unless either an engine or brake van is at the Hardengreen end of the wagons.'

market centre for the farmsteads and hamlets strung along the south eastern slopes of the Pentland Hills. It was also on the fringe of the Lothian coalfield, although local reserves had hardly been touched by the mid-nineteenth century. Furthermore, there were mills alongside the river and its lovely surroundings gave the town great potential as a residential area for Edinburgh's professionals. Although the Caledonian was still hankering after a line along the North Esk valley, this particular prize went to a local company.

The Penicuik Railway was authorised on 20th June 1870 and opened for goods and passenger traffic on 9th May and 2nd September 1872 respectively. It left the Peebles Railway at Hawthornden Junction and immediately descended steeply into the valley, carving a shelf through rough wooded ground. Rosslyn Castle station (three quarters of a mile from the junction) was in a beautiful setting with the red sandstone pile of Roslin Castle peering out of the trees above the far bank and Roslin itself in the distance. A little way beyond the sizeable goods yard the track was covered by an iron and timber shed, known oddly as the 'tin tunnel', installed to prevent sparks causing a catastrophe at the gunpowder works down in Roslin Glen. More earthworks on the precipitous slope down to the North Esk followed and led to a fascinating half mile stretch of railway. First came a

graceful ten arch stone viaduct curving over a great amphitheatre surrounded by trees. A skew plate-girder bridge over a trackway followed the westernmost arch and the line was soon back on a shelf high above the rushing water. After a couple of hundred yards it plunged into a sharply

curved tunnel through an abrupt spur, followed by yet another shelf. This led to a flattish area dominated by the large Dalmore paper mill, although a modest girder bridge over Glencorse Burn was required during this brief transect. A second tunnel took the rails under the Milton to Howgate road and a neat bowstring girder bridge over the North Esk came immediately afterwards. By now the river was just a few feet below track level, such was the gradient of the valley floor. Auchendinny station (two miles) had a long curved platform and a short goods bay squeezed between the turbulent stream and a steep slope. A ninety degree curve and two more river crossings led to Eskbridge station (three miles) which opened on 1st July 1874 and stood near a superbly built skew brick and stone arch carrying a minor road. By now the valley side was so severe that a hefty stone retaining wall was needed to support rock and earth above the permanent way. With the line climbing at this point, the North Esk was some way below the rails once again and another mill peered up from the far bank. After a fifth river crossing the valley opened out at last and the branch reached its terminus on the southern edge of Penicuik - but not before the waters had been diverted under the track and back again on the edge of a large mill complex. Somewhat remarkably, the branch finished up at just below 550ft above sea level, the same altitude at which it began. The Penicuik Railway, worked by the North British from the outset, and was amalgamated with the larger company on 13th July 1876.

Penicuik was a desirable goal and the Edinburgh, Loanhead & Roslin Railway,

Although the waiting room had been demolished, closed Broomieknowe station was otherwise complete on 7th March 1959. In this view looking towards Polton, the solid stone bridge carrying Broomieknowe High Street is clearly visible. The cutting is partially filled in and now forms a walkway through the Eldindean and Quarryhead districts of Bonnyrigg towards Lothian Street. Even relatively obscure stations such as this saw special workings during the 1930s, one example being a Broomieknowe Churches outing to Gullane.

also authorised on 20th June 1870, aimed to reach it as well. After much squabbling with the Penicuik Railway and the threat of legal action, the former decided to go no further than Roslin, which in any case had the best coal reserves. Although the chosen route kept to high ground on the north west shoulder of the North Esk valley, it had to cross a deep gorge carved by Bilston Burn, a tributary of the main river. This took some bridging and hampered the completion of the line. Mineral traffic from Loanhead began on 6th November 1873 but passenger and goods services to Roslin had to wait until 23rd July 1874. The North British urged the Edinburgh, Loanhead & Roslin to complete its authorised route to Penicuik, but the company had lost interest in the town and decided to venture only as far as Greenlaw Barracks, to tap more coal seams. This modest extension was authorised on 5th August 1873 and opened on 2nd July 1877. On 1st December 1877 the new terminus was renamed Glencorse and eventually a further extension to Penicuik gasworks brought the line to within three quarters of a mile of the town centre.

The single track Edinburgh, Loanhead & Roslin line left the Waverley route at Millerhill just over 150ft above sea level. It curved sharply westwards and climbed steadily through featureless country reaching 250ft at Todhills and 350ft at Gilmerton station (two and a quarter miles from the junction). After following the gentle Park Burn valley for a mile or so, the rails veered south and cut through a ridge at Edgefield to reach Loanhead (four and a quarter miles) on the 450ft contour. A lowly passage through the middle of the village and excavations through another minor spur brought the formation to Bilston Glen. This was a formidable obstacle, for the lively Bilston Burn had descended to almost 300ft at this point and its valley was steep sided and heavily wooded. Brick piers were thrust upwards from the sheer

Lasswade, now overshadowed by nearby Bonnyrigg, is an attractive little village where the Dalkeith to Loanhead road bridged the North Esk. It has literary associations with Sir Walter Scott but the character of the place was hardly reflected by its station on the Esk Valley Railway. Although the company spent a lot of money constructing its short line to Polton, passenger facilities were meagre to say the least. Lasswade was provided with a fairly short platform on a curve and a mean brick building with a glazed timber frontage to the waiting room. Framed by the tunnel mouth more than seven years after passenger services ceased, Lasswade station was gently decaying on 7th March 1959. The site is now occupied by a road serving a new housing estate, but the blocked up tunnel mouth and fenced off viaduct may still be seen. During the 1930s excursion bonanza Lasswade was the destination for a Bakery Workers Union trip from Waverley.

Polton nestles in splendid isolation down by the North Esk and is a world apart from nearby Loanhead and Bonnyrigg on the airy shoulders of the valley, but the railway revitalised this remote village and stimulated its industry. The last vestige of this activity was being carried out on 24th May 1962 as class J35 No.64510 collected three vans from the local paper mill before heading back to Hardengreen yard. Polton had a short single platform with a rather mean building in yellow brick, although this was relieved by a large canopy which can just be seen beyond the brake van. In May 1930 seven trains each way provided a link with Edinburgh taking about 28 minutes and there were still five return workings in May 1948. Traditionally, the first departure from the village headed for Leith Central.

Deep in the North Esk valley near the grounds of New Saughton Hall, class J35 0-6-0 No.64510 propelled a brake van, en route from Hardengreen yard to Polton, across the river on 24th May 1962. This was the second and more modest crossing of the North Esk. The spectacular viaduct taking the line from the south to north bank was less than half a mile away off to the right and a fine aerial view of it can still be obtained from the Rosewell to Lasswade road.

Ex-North British 0-4-4T No.9334 at Polton with a train for Edinburgh Waverley on 26th May 1937, typifying many passenger services on the Southern Branches in the LNER years. Twelve of these Reid 0-4-4Ts were built in 1909, the last of this wheel arrangement built for the NBR. As LNER class G9, they went for scrap between 1936 and 1940, No.9334 being withdrawn early in 1939. Photograph National Railway Museum.

In marked contrast to its heavy engineering works up the North Esk Valley, the Penicuik Railway adopted a modest local style for its station houses. Those at Rosslyn Castle and Auchendinny were like little cottage and both of them have been converted into homes which blend perfectly with the surrounding dwellings. Even Penicuik had a tiny amenities block for passengers, although this was overshadowed by a substantial goods shed. The moribund terminus was complete and the adjacent mills were still providing goods traffic when this view was taken on 20th January 1962. The bridge in the background carried Peebles Road over a branch to Valleyfield Mill which survives as a council depot and engineering works. The site was shunted by a pug, since preserved by the Lytham Motive Power Museum. Constricted access through the arch led the North British to issue an instruction that 'covered vans cannot be dealt with at Valleyfield Mill.' Esk Paper Mills also had two shunting engines, which worked until rail traffic ceased with the closure of the branch. The station itself and the huge mills off to the right have been demolished and the site attractively landscaped.

slopes to accommodate wrought iron lattice girders, the finished structure being 166 yards long and 150ft high in the middle. Gentler country took the line to the attractive village of Roslin (six and a quarter miles from Millerhill and 500ft up) where the branch terminated for three years. The extension to Glencorse (seven and three quarter miles) was dominated by the beautiful Pentland Hills just two miles away and featured a sixteen arch brick viaduct across the broad Glencorse Burn valley, just short of the new terminus. A further extension to Penicuik gasworks and Eastfield Colliery took the line up to almost 600ft.

From the 1870s to the early 1920s the North Esk railways were virtually lifelines for the small communities south of Edinburgh. Passenger trains were the only realistic way of travelling to and from the city and plenty of wagon loads left mines, mills and loading bays. World War I economies forced the closure of Broomieknowe and Eskbridge, from 1st January 1917 to 1st April 1919 and 2nd June 1919 respectively. Ten years later buses and lorries were beginning to have an impact and Eskbridge closed to all traffic on 22nd September 1930. Passenger services on the Glencorse line ceased on 1st May 1933 despite the conveniently located stations at Loanhead and Roslin. World War II delayed the inevitable retrenchment, but British Railways discarded the Polton and Penicuik passenger trains on 10th September 1951, having abandoned all traffic at Auchendinny six months previously, on 5th March. Public goods facilities at Gilmerton, Roslin and Glencorse were withdrawn on 1st July 1959, although the first two still had traffic from nearby collieries. The rural goods yard at Rosslyn Castle closed on 3rd August 1959 and freight trains on the Polton branch ceased on 18th May 1964. Penicuik goods traffic finished on 27th March 1967 and parcels facilities at Loanhead were withdrawn on 22nd July 1968. The closure of Bilston Glen colliery in 1993 meant the very end for the North Esk lines.

Below right:- With the crew and station staff posing for the photographer, an ex-North British J36 0-6-0 stood at Glencorse with the pick up goods during the late 1930s. A couple of basic red brick buildings with sloping roofs, familiar cream brick relief and a timber waiting room between them formed the actual passenger facilities, although a large two storey house at right angles to the platform added a touch of substance to the station. The branch service comprised just four trains each way in May 1930, half of them running to and from Millerhill where Edinburgh connections were provided by Polton, Penicuik or Dalkeith workings. There was almost an eight hour gap in Glencorse departures, from 8.02am to 3.58pm. Three extras each way ran on Saturdays, including a 10.45pm from Waverley. Photograph National Railway Museum.

Roslin station stood on the northern edge of the attractive Esk valley village and provided a lovely view of the Pentland Hills. It is seen here on 7th March 1959 nearly 26 years after closure. With the exception of Loanhead, stations on the Edinburgh, Loanhead & Roslin Railway displayed a common style featuring basic yet pleasant buildings in dark brown brick with cream brick relief around windows and doorways. All traces of the passenger facilities at Roslin have disappeared although a delightful little goods office still exists on the opposite side of the Bilston road. The site of Glencorse station has also been obliterated, by new houses and a car park opposite the barracks. However, in a remote spot some way from the dour brown sandstone village of Gilmerton, a large station house survives as a tangible reminder of the architectural characteristics adopted by the long dissolved company.

The Edinburgh, Loanhead & Roslin Railway served Loanhead very well, for the station was in the middle of this large village. Despite an early demise in 1933, the facilities were still virtually complete in 1994 and a very faded painted sign 'Ticket Office' could even be discerned. A small plain building with a low pitched roof stood parallel to the track. It was constructed of second rate red and yellow bricks, although the platform side had a fairly intricate timber screen wall. Immediately alongside was a quaint station house with an extremely steep roof and '1874' prominent on one of the walls. An attractive bargeboard finished off the gable end facing the platform. On 21st October 1963 class J37 0-6-0 No.64624 left Loanhead with a loaded coal train from Ramsay Colliery to Millerhill Yard. The mine, closed in 1965, is prominent on the right.

With the crew and station staff posing for the photographer, an ex-North British J36 0-6-0 stood at Glencorse with the pick up goods during the late 1930s.

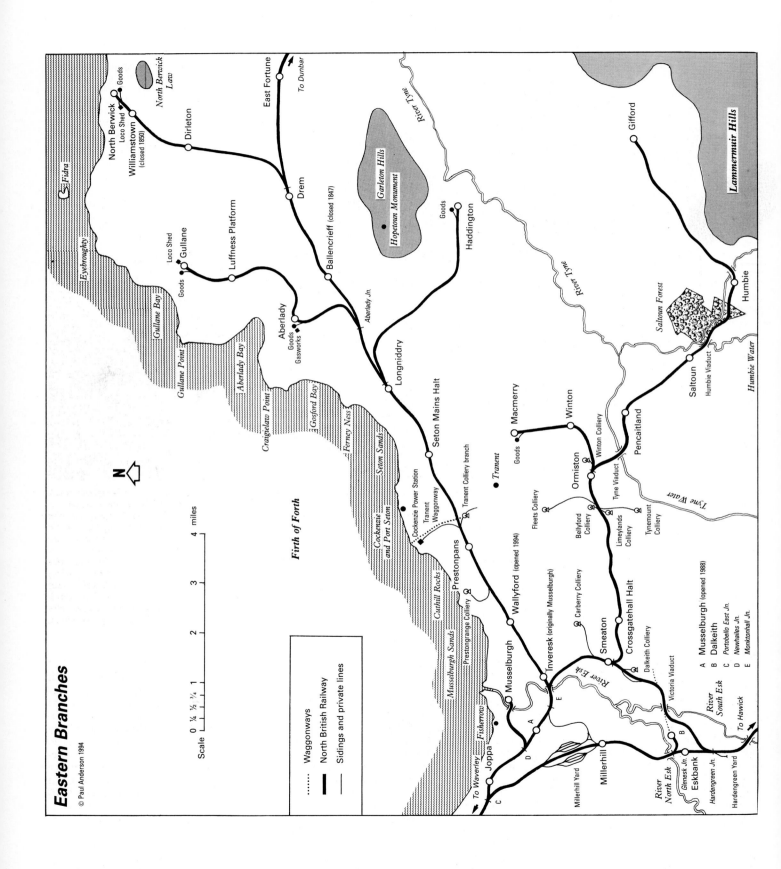

Eastern Branches

© Paul Anderson 1994

Waggonways

North British Railway

Sidings and private lines

Scale

0 ¼ ½ ¾ 1   2   3   4 miles

Firth of Forth

N

North Berwick Law

Goods — North Berwick
Loco Shed
Williamstown (closed 1850)
Dirleton
East Fortune
To Dunbar
Drem
Ballencrieff (closed 1847)
Loco Shed — Gullane
Goods
Luffness Platform
Aberlady
Goods
Gasworks
Aberlady Jn.
Longniddry
Seton Mains Halt
River Tyne
Garleton Hills
Hopetoun Monument
Goods
Haddington
River Tyne
Saltoun Forest
Gifford
Lammermuir Hills
Humbie
Saltoun
Humbie Viaduct
Humbie Water
Pencaitland
Winton Colliery
Winton
Macmerry
Goods
Ormiston
Tyne Viaduct
Limeylands Colliery
Tynemount Colliery
Tyne Water
Bellyford Colliery
Fleets Colliery
Trent
Tranent Colliery branch
Tranent Waggonway
Cockenzie Power Station
Cockenzie and Port Seton
Seton Sands
Ferney Ness
Gosford Bay
Craigielaw Point
Aberlady Bay
Gullane Point
Gullane Bay
Eyebroughty
Fidra
Prestonpans
Prestongrange Colliery
Cuthill Rocks
Wallyford (opened 1994)
Carberry Colliery
Smeaton
Crossgatehall Halt
Dalkeith Colliery
Victoria Viaduct
Inveresk (originally Musselburgh)
Musselburgh (opened 1988)
Musselburgh
River Esk
Musselburgh Sands
Fisherrow
To Waverley
Joppa
Millerhill
Millerhill Yard
Eskbank
River North Esk
River South Esk
Hardengreen Jn.
Hardengreen Yard
Glenesk Jn.
To Hawick

A Musselburgh
B Dalkeith
C Portobello East Jn.
D Newhailes Jn.
E Monktonhall Jn.

Chapter Five
Eastern Branches

Haddington station stood on a steep slope overlooking the main Edinburgh road and its original building was a simple affair with pleasant Tudor touches, presenting a single storey to the platform and two storeys to the driveway. During the 1880s the embankment and platform were extended to accommodate a new structure. This in essence followed the contemporary North British style, but the combination of an awkward site and extra embellishments led to a remarkable creation. From the platform side it was a lengthy single storey block with a longitudinal gabled roof and a generous canopy. However, from the road approach it towered above its surroundings and faced Haddington with a bold gable end featuring a large clock. The main exterior elevation had repetitive round-headed windows at the upper level and a projecting central section finished off with another gable. The lower part of the wall, which both supported the structure and contained the embankment, featured a series of blind arches and recesses, the symmetry being disrupted by sloping ground and a rather fine covered stairway of timber and glass. A striking combination of brownish-red bricks and white brick relief was used to considerable effect. The main gables featured heavy fretwork bargeboards capped by little finials whilst delicate ironwork completed the ridge tiles. Decorative iron railings between five massive red sandstone pillars supporting ornate lamps bordered the pavement. This fine view of the striking edifice was taken on 19th April 1913. Photograph W.F. Jackson, Glasgow University Archives.

E ast of the Waverley route the beautiful and varied country side of East Lothian stretches away towards the North Sea coast. Just beyond Dalkeith it was once a hive of mining activity, but the pits soon gave way to a broad coastal plain which has long been the richest cereal growing area in Scotland. To the south the River Tyne and its tributaries drain well wooded uplands rising steadily to the Lammermuir Hills, a stretch of wild moorland reaching 1,755ft at Meikle Says Law. To the north the farmland merges with a coastline of sand dunes, glorious bays and golf courses. Added interest is provided by the sudden volcanic outcrops forming prominent hills such as Traprain

Law, or rugged islands like Bass Rock. The North British main line passed through the northern edge of East Lothian in a sweeping arc, often within sight of the sea. Between 1846 and 1901 five branches sprang directly, or in the last case, indirectly, from the East Coast main line and they were just as varied as the landscape. One of them has retained a passenger service for nearly a century and a half whilst the booking offices on another were open for just 32 years.

The first feeder line served the county town of Haddington, a particularly attractive place with wide streets and fine 18th century buildings. In marked contrast, the terminus eventually gained one of the most garish examples of North Brit-

ish architecture to be found in the Edinburgh area. Shortly afterwards, North Berwick was reached by another short branch. This pleasant seaside town has kept its passenger trains despite a serious threat in the late 1960s and elderly electric multiple units displaced from the London area now operate the very successful service. The village of Macmerry was an unlikely terminus for a branch line, but it was the prospect of coal traffic which provided the impetus for construction. Passenger services to Macmerry ceased seventy years ago, although mineral trains continued to use much of the route until comparatively recently. Gullane on the coast west of North Berwick was the next village to

Gatepost and lamp at Haddington

After the small 0-4-2s which worked the branch in its early years, North Berwick saw a succession of 0-6-0, 4-4-0 and 0-4-4 tanks. In LNER years C16 4-4-2Ts were regular performers, although Sentinel steam railcars were tried and Gresley N2 0-6-2Ts, then V1 2-6-2Ts proved powerful alternatives during the 1930s. The C16s continued to show up in early BR days and No.67495 arrived at North Berwick on 1st May 1954 with the 4.31pm from Drem. This short line can boast a history unique on Britain's railways. Not only has it experienced horse traction, conventional steam power, steam railcars, first generation diesel multiple units, Sprinters and class 158s, but has also carried a named restaurant car express, been threatened with closure and is now electrified.

Gresley N2 0-6-2T No.4727 at Drem with a North Berwick to Edinburgh Waverley morning business train some time during the late 1920s or early 1930s. The polished buffers and thistles etched into the smokebox door were no doubt the work of men at North Berwick shed (sub to St. Margarets) where one of these engines was allocated for duties on the branch. Over forty N2s were transferred to Scotland between 1925 and 1929, initially to St. Margarets, Haymarket, Dundee, Dunfermline, Glasgow and the Borders. No.4727 was built in 1920 by the North British Locomotive Company of Glasgow and operated suburban services out of London King's Cross for a time. The N2s proved heavy on the permanent way in Scotland and were restricted to 40mph on the North Berwick branch. Photograph J.J. Cunningham.

The Gresley 2-6-2Ts proved highly successful on Edinburgh local routes and V1 No.67659 was ready for a sprightly run to Waverley as it waited at North Berwick with the 6.13pm departure on 1st May 1954. The booked time to Drem was down to eight minutes by the late 1930s when there were up to nineteen trains each way, and a similar schedule applied in the early 1950s with a somewhat reduced timetable of thirteen return workings. The complex curved double scissors trackwork for engine release purposes is clearly visible in this view. North Berwick originally had a single platform with a modest station house, but complete reconstruction during 1894 produced a rather large terminus with two long platforms and extensive timber fronted buildings featuring large windows. Fine canopies with low chamfered roofs and deep valances were supported on cast iron columns with decorative spandrels, whilst a graceful curved canopy overlooked the exterior courtyard. Wholesale demolition of the decaying Victorian structures in 1985, accompanied by a drastic shortening of the remaining platform, inevitably destroyed the character of the place but at least at long-closed Dirleton the station house, with its absurdly tall chimneys, can still be seen.

The hourly diesel multiple unit service between North Berwick and Corstorphine came into operation on 3rd February 1958 and typical of such workings was this Gloucester twin set, forming the 10.22am departure from Corstorphine, seen arriving at its East Lothian destination on 24th May 1962. The roof of the disused loco shed is prominent in the left foreground. North Berwick goods yard was quite extensive and had a fan of ten sidings as well as a substantial brick transit shed. In its heyday the depot handled a large amount of agricultural traffic as well as substantial quantities of fish, but the site is now occupied by houses. In the far corner of the yard are Pullman Camping Coaches Nos.42 and 46, the latter once a South Eastern and Chatham Railway vehicle originally built for the Folkestone Boat Trains. They were awaiting transfer to Gullane where they spent a season before returning to North Berwick for disposal. The Derby three car units in the station had formed a special for a BR staff outing from Glasgow Queen Street and were the latest example of the excursion traffic which had ventured down the branch from its early days.

gain a railway, the aim being to develop residential traffic. In reality it became very much a line for leisure, especially golf. Finally, the charming village of Gifford, on the edge of the Lammermuir Hills, was reached by a very rural branch from Ormiston on the Macmerry line. It was particularly vulnerable to road transport and the passenger service had a very short life.

HADDINGTON AND NORTH BERWICK

East Lothian was originally Haddingtonshire and the royal burgh which once administered the county is one of the most dignified towns in Scotland. Haddington was established a thousand years ago and several periods of its subsequent history were violent; the town was burned by the English on a couple of occasions and was held by them against the Scots and French in 1548-49. Previously, religious establishments were dominant and an impressive reminder of these early times is St. Mary's Church, the 'Lamp of Lothian' which dates from the 13th and 15th centuries and overlooks the River Tyne near the site of a Cistercian nunnery. However, most buildings reflect Haddington's more recent role as a wealthy market centre for the East Lothian grain growers and a stagecoach

stop on the Great North Road. Such prosperity might have led to complacency, but local worthies were quick to realise the potential impact of new trunk railways and urged, indeed expected, the North British to build its Edinburgh - Berwick line through the town. With gentle gradients of paramount importance, the tracks were laid some three and a half miles to the north and served the villages of Longniddry and Drem instead. After much lobbying, Haddington was granted a branch from Longniddry, and this was authorised and opened at the same time as the main line - on 4th July 1844 and 22nd June 1846 respectively. Through coaches to Edinburgh and convenient connections for Berwick were promised, and it seemed at the time that plenty of traffic would be forthcoming.

From about 100ft above sea level at Longniddry, the Haddington branch ran parallel to the Berwick route for three quarters of a mile before veering away at 1 in 66 on a sweeping embankment up the hillside. A cutting through a wooded spur near Setonhill followed, the tracks topping 250ft at Laverocklaw by which time a splendid panorama of the Firth of Forth could be enjoyed from the carriage windows. The line reached its summit (at just over 300ft) in a cutting through a ridge just beyond Merryhatton. This was

three miles from Longniddry and marked the beginning of a steady fall at 1 in 80 down the gentle slopes of the Back Burn valley. Pleasant glimpses of the Garleton Hills and the Napoleonic Hopetown Memorial enhanced the descent towards the Tyne valley and Haddington station at 200ft. Unfortunately the terminus was inconveniently sited on rising ground almost three quarters of a mile west of the town centre and a horse bus provided connections to and from the trains. The branch was doubled towards the end of 1846, seemingly because of a threat from the proposed East Lothian & Tyne Valley Railway, which would have provided a station in the middle of Haddington. This particular 'Railway Mania' scheme came to nought and as traffic proved far lighter than predicted, single track working was reinstated during October 1856. At first there were five trains a day in each direction; they were allowed fifteen minutes for the journey, but most of them only carried a handful of passengers. Eventually loadings rose to a reasonable level before plummeting again as a result of motor bus competition. Rather surprisingly, the line had a modest Sunday service from the outset and retained it until the end. The Haddington branch experienced a long yet rather unremarkable career. Perhaps the most interesting de-

Although it stood at the fairly modest altitude of 200ft, Smeaton station commanded fine views of the coastal plain, Arthur's Seat and the Firth of Forth to the north and the Pentland Hills away to the west. It had an odd little island platform almost as broad as it was long and two rather primitive brick buildings with hipped roofs, projecting timbers at the eaves and simple windows and doorways. A large water tower dominated the southern end. In this view looking south, J36 0-6-0 No.65345 runs round the stock of an SLS rail tour on 27th August 1966. The Macmerry line climbed away up the hillside on the left, whilst the Hardengreen Junction tracks went straight ahead. Dalkeith Colliery in the background closed during 1978. Most of the station site is now wasteland although the platform, with its rough timber edging can still be seen. Specials were also a feature in the 1930s, after the passenger service ceased. On a particularly busy day there was a Sunday school outing conveying some 200 adults and 650 children from Leith Central to Ormiston, whilst that afternoon a somewhat more modest complement of about 40 passengers arrived by steam coach from Portobello. The Sentinel then retired to St. Margarets shed and its patrons were required to squeeze aboard the Leith Central train for the return journey! The same day there was a special from Morningside Road to Winton for 200 adults and 350 children.

Ormiston station was completely different from Smeaton and had a single platform of reasonable length. The pleasant little building in red brick with cream brick relief had a gabled block at right angles to the platform, a longer wing parallel to the track, and a timber fronted waiting room. On 11th June 1960 J35 0-6-0 No.64489 paused at Ormiston in charge of the SLS 'East Lothian Excursion' with the loco water tank prominent in the foreground. Agricultural land with a sprinkling of trees forms much of the background but this was also mining country and the spoil heap of Fleets Colliery can be seen in the distance behind North Mains Farm. Another pit once stood next to the station, near the sidings occupied by box vans.

velopment was the reconstruction of the terminus during the 1880s, when an impressive but rather unusual building, totally out of keeping with the town, was erected.

North Berwick nestles around a natural harbour midway along the broad peninsula which thrusts into the Firth of Forth between Longniddry and Dunbar. It is a comfortable and easy-going little resort and is dominated by the 613ft volcanic North Berwick Law. Like Haddington, the town has long been a royal burgh and can also claim a history stretching back some ten centuries. In the 1840s its harbour was an expanse of silt at low tide, though the pier had a weekly sailing from Leith, bringing in coal and taking away agricultural produce. Fishing boats ventured out to find the herring shoals and the wealthy had just discovered its merits as a place to seabathe and play golf. With a population of over 1,600 it was the only coastal settlement of any size not served by the North British main line and had to be content with a horse bus connection from Drem at first. On 16th June 1846, just six days before its regular service from Edinburgh to Berwick began, the North British obtained an Act for a branch from Drem to North Berwick harbour. Considering the parlous financial state of the company, this was regarded as an act of folly by some observers. Nevertheless construction work, through sometimes difficult terrain, went ahead and the line opened

as far as a temporary wooden platform near Williamstown Farm, just short of North Berwick, on 13th August 1849. The four and a half mile branch was completed to the town on 17th June 1850 and Williamstown closed, although an intermediate halt purporting to serve Dirleton opened in the middle of nowhere on the same date. After second thoughts about the expense and likely usage, the harbour extension was abandoned.

Having left the main line at Drem, some 80ft above sea level, the branch curved northwards and descended gently at 1 in 110 over fairly featureless ground affording views of Gullane on its sandhills away to the left. An embankment then took the track over Peffer Burn and Mill Burn towards East Fenton with North Berwick Law appearing in the distance beyond clumps of woodland on low hills. A climb at 1 in 93 up to the 100ft contour led to a sheer cutting through volcanic rock, followed by another embankment. By now North Berwick Law was becoming very prominent and contrasted markedly with the expanse of grain fields stretching down to the sea. Beyond Dirleton station (two and a half miles from Drem) the rails veered eastwards and into another cutting through an outcrop of igneous rock, though this time the sides were less severe. A short descent at 1 in 66 brought the branch to its terminus 70ft above sea level and slightly less than half a mile from the town centre. In 1849 there were four trains a day each

way, with a horse bus providing connections between Williamstown and High Street, and this level of service continued after North Berwick station opened, the journey time to Drem being about twenty minutes. The North British encouraged Edinburgh businessmen to build high class villas near the station but the response was disappointing. As a result trains were running at a loss, so with cost cutting in mind the steam service was replaced from 1st November 1856 by a horse drawn stagecoach-like vehicle known as DANDY NO.1. Its lethargic progress to the junction caused an outcry and savings were not that great, so locomotives made a welcome return on 1st May 1857. By this time North Berwick was becoming a popular holiday resort for Edinburgh and goods traffic was flourishing as well. Eventually the anticipated residential development did take place and commuter services began to thrive. By 1880 there were eight branch trains each way taking seventeen minutes, but in 1900 the service was up to eleven return workings timed at ten minutes between North Berwick and Drem, several of them through services to and from Edinburgh Waverley. On 3rd June 1912 the prestigious 'Lothian Coast Express' from Dunbar, North Berwick and Gullane was inaugurated, a long awaited manifestation of the elite business travel envisaged in the late 1840s. As with Haddington, increasing traffic at North Berwick warranted better passenger fa-

Yet another style was employed for the terminus at Macmerry although it did have a slight affinity with the structures at Smeaton. The simple brick building had a shallow hipped roof with very prominent overhangs at the eaves. In this early 1930s study the station had a very woebegone look about it, passenger services having ceased in 1925. Today all signs of the platform have disappeared under a huge mound of earth, but there are traces of the goods loading bay, which was off to the left. This is still an exposed, breezy, spot with fine views on a clear day. Macmerry itself retains numerous rows of single storey cottages built for miners in Victorian times and now attractively modernised. One block - on the opposite side of the main A1 road which ran behind the fence in the right of this view - bears the name Station Row, thus commemorating the long-abandoned passenger service. Photograph Scottish Record Office.

cilities and the improved terminus opened in March 1894. There were no physical problems with the site and the buildings were solid and extensive, if rather dull.

The North Berwick and Haddington branches had much in common for many years, especially regarding residential traffic to Edinburgh, but their respective careers began to diverge under LNER ownership and could hardly present a greater contrast today. North Berwick commuter traffic held up well and the line was very busy with excursionists in the summer. Haddington trains, however, were attracting fewer and fewer customers as the town took to its frequent bus services along the Great North Road. World War II only delayed the inevitable and passenger facilities were withdrawn on 4th December 1949. Dirleton station closed to passengers on 1st February 1954 and it is astonishing that it survived for so long.

Early in 1958 diesel multiple units took over North Berwick workings and the small loco shed just outside the terminus became redundant. Goods traffic on the two lines was abandoned during the next decade. Dirleton yard closed on 1st August 1964, North Berwick lost its facilities on 1st January 1968 and the Haddington branch closed completely on 30th March 1968. The North Berwick passenger service soon came under threat as well, but after a spirited campaign it was reprieved in the autumn of 1969. Regular electric services to Edinburgh

began on 8th July 1991 in the wake of the East Coast scheme and in 1994 there were seventeen trains each way taking just seven minutes to and from Drem. Meanwhile, the Haddington branch had been converted into a pleasant footpath known as the 'Railway Walk'.

MACMERRY, GULLANE AND GIFFORD

East of Dalkeith and Inveresk the ground climbs rapidly to form a prominent north-south ridge, reaching almost 500ft at Falside Hill and Queen Mary's Mount and rising to over 600ft near Fordel. It marked the eastern edge of the Lothian coalfield and several pits were sunk in the area during early Victorian times. Production increased steadily and with the whole-hearted support of most landowners, the North British proposed an extension of its system to tap the collieries. This was duly sanctioned on 3rd June 1862 and comprised a through line from Monktonhall Junction on the East Coast main line near Inveresk, to Hardengreen Junction on the Waverley route south of Dalkeith, together with a branch from Smeaton to the industrial village of Macmerry near Tranent. The former utilised the route of the Duke of Buccleuch's tramway, including Victoria viaduct, for its alignment north of Dalkeith. Construction was a leisurely process and the new railways opened for mineral traffic in stages, finally reaching Macmerry on 19th March 1868 and Hardengreen Junction

on 31st July 1870. During the planning stage there were optimistic utterings of a passenger service from Edinburgh to Hawick and the Esk Valley via a new station in Dalkeith, but this never came to fruition. Eventually, stations opened at Smeaton, Ormiston, Winton and Macmerry on 1st May 1872 - almost ten years after the lines were authorised - and a halt at Crossgatehall followed on 1st August 1913. The service was both sparse and dilatory. Just three return workings a day ventured from Edinburgh to Macmerry and they averaged less than 20mph. At the turn of the century even the midday train was withdrawn on weekdays.

From Monktonhall Junction just over 50ft above sea level, the Macmerry line headed southwards and climbed steeply out of the Esk valley on a substantial embankment, part of which was on a fairly sharp curve. Smeaton station (a mile and a half from the junction) was well above the 150ft contour and served a couple of farms, but not much else. By almost doubling back on itself up the hillside the branch then veered eastwards and carved its way through the ridge between Queen Mary's Mount and Fordel in a very deep rock cutting at Cousland Gap. Crossgatehall Halt (two and a half miles from Monktonhall and well over 250ft up) was in the middle of this excavation. The summit just east of here exceeded 300ft and an almost imperceptible descent along the broad Elphinstone valley followed. Ormiston station was just north of the pleasant farming village alongside the trickling headwaters of the River Tyne. A gentle passage, first eastwards then northwards, lifted the line across well wooded farmland through remote Winton station (seven miles) and eventually to Macmerry, eight miles from Monktonhall, on exposed tableland 300ft above the Firth of Forth. The Hardengreen line pushed southwards from Smeaton to Thorneybank on the edge of Dalkeith, then crossed the South Esk by means of the six-arch Victoria viaduct which was rebuilt with lattice girder deck spans on modified masonry piers. A winding passage through the eastern edge of the town, partially in a cutting, then led the rails to the Hawick route. Although the timetable at Smeaton and Ormiston improved when the Gifford branch opened, villages east of Inveresk and Dalkeith were poorly served by the passenger trains. Goods traffic - especially coal - was prolific however, and over thirty collieries and other industrial sites had access to the Macmerry and Hardengreen Junction lines over the years.

The attractive shoreline between Longniddry and North Berwick is a succession of rocky headlands and sandy bays with intriguing names like Kilspindie and Bubbly Buss. Three settlements, each with its own distinctive character, are strung along this coastal margin of the peninsula. Aberlady at the mouth of the Peffer Burn was Haddington's port and the bay was once busy with sailing vessels; Gullane stood in the lee of 200ft sand dunes and became synonymous with golf, a game originally introduced to Scotland from Holland during the 1400s; Dirleton, clustered around its ruined 13th century castle, has often been described as the most beautiful village north of the border. However, the East Coast main line together with its associated offshoots to Haddington and North Berwick left them somewhat isolated, leading to a period of stagnation. Local interests wanted their own branch railway and with strong North British backing the Aberlady, Gullane & North Berwick Railway received its Act of Parliament on 24th August 1893. Construction was again fairly lethargic but the line eventually opened as far as Gullane on 1st April 1898. A generous service of nine passenger trains each way was provided and there were several extras on Saturdays. Flocks of summer visitors began to arrive by train, golf flourished, and the revival of the coastal villages began in earnest. The local company surrendered its independence to the North British on 6th August 1900 and a private halt for golfers opened at Luffness on 1st September 1903, yet there was still no sign of the extension to North Berwick. A railway-owned charabanc plugged the gap (calling at Dirleton on the way) from June 1905 to

September 1910 and right up to World War I there was occasional pressure for the line to be completed. Gullane however was destined to remain the terminus until the line closed.

From Aberlady Junction, a mile and a half east of Longniddry and just over 100ft above sea level, the single track branch ran alongside the main line for a quarter of a mile, gradually losing height. It then veered northwards on a low embankment before dropping below 50ft near Ballencrieff Mains and continued across open farmland dotted with spinneys to Aberlady station, three miles from Longniddry. This was about half a mile south of the village, next to the Haddington road overbridge, and stood on a sweeping 150 degree curve which slewed the alignment eastwards. A more gradual curve through fields and woodland near Luffness Mains followed and the rails were heading north again. By Luffness Platform (four and three quarter miles) close to a bridge across Peffer Burn, the branch was just a few feet above sea level. A gentle ascent past Saltcoates Castle to the east and acres of golf links on rising ground to the west brought the railway within sight of Gullane and above the 50ft contour again. With another change of direction the branch turned north eastwards and entered a cutting before spreading out to occupy a sizeable tract of land for its terminal arrangements, six and a quarter miles from Longniddry. Local trains were hauled by 0-6-0 tender

engines or 0-4-4 and 4-4-2 tanks, whilst through Edinburgh workings, including the 'Lothian Coast Express', were often in the capable hands of 4-4-0s. Gullane expanded rapidly in late Victorian and Edwardian years, acquiring hotels, numerous large villas and new golf courses. Having precipitated this boom, the local railway shared the prosperity and for a quarter of a century the trains were very busy, especially in summer.

The last of Edinburgh's eastern branches was one of those delightful light railways more associated with remote rural areas than the catchment area of a major city. Gifford, some eighteen miles east of the capital and nestling in the foothills of the Lammermuirs, was specially laid out during the 17th and 18th centuries to meet the needs of workers on the large Yester House estate. Its main street is dominated by the attractive whitewashed kirk dating from 1708, and around the corner a broad green marking the beginning of a driveway to Yester House is bordered by two storey cottages with red pantile roofs in best East Lothian tradition. Although much of Britain was reaping the benefits of railway communication by late Victorian times, several well populated agricultural districts were still some way from a railhead and were handicapped as a consequence. This certainly applied to the area south of Haddington and moves to counter the isolation began in 1889 when a branch from Haddington was mooted. Nothing came

The eastern branches had a tendency to creep away from the main line almost apologetically rather than striking away with confidence. This applied particularly to the Aberlady, Gullane & North Berwick, which clung to the East Coast route for several hundred yards. With Aberlady Junction box visible in the background and the Gullane track losing height on the right, Deltic D9010 KING'S OWN SCOTTISH BORDERER boomed down the 1 in 300 towards Ballencrieff with the up 'Queen of Scots' Pullman to London King's Cross on 24th August 1963. The train had left Glasgow Queen Street at 11.00am.

of it, although a North British branch to Garvald via Gifford was authorised in 1891, only to be superseded by a proposal two years later, for a line just to Gifford. After plenty of talk but precious little action, it was left to the Light Railway Commissioners to rescue this part of Haddingtonshire when the Gifford & Garvald Railway Act was passed on 14th July 1898. Construction work began nine months later and trains began running from Ormiston to Gifford on 14th October 1901. Meanwhile the extension to Garvald was quietly forgotten.

Attractive scenery was characteristic of the line throughout its nine and a quarter miles, but it was laid against the grain of the country and three summits together with no less than forty changes of gradient were necessary. Over half the route consisted of vicious 1 in 50 inclines, whilst two viaducts and numerous earthworks had to be provided. From about 270ft at Ormiston the single track curved southwards and dropped slightly before crossing a three span viaduct over Tyne Water. A minor summit in a curved cutting at Kiloran was followed by another slight dip, then the short ascent to Pencaitland station (a mile and three quarters from Ormiston and still about 300ft up). By Lempock the branch had

climbed to 400ft but dropped again to Kinchie Burn and Saltoun station (three and a half miles). Swelling hillslopes capped by woodland were closing in by now and the distant Lammermuirs formed a grey skyline. A two and a half mile climb mainly at 1 in 50, taking the line across Humbie Water on a four arch masonry viaduct and past the mysterious gloom of Saltoun Forest. Humbie station, five and a half miles from Ormiston and no less than two and a quarter from the hamlet it purported to serve, was almost on the 500ft contour. Having headed more or less south eastwards all the way from Pencaitland, the track was now faced with the steep northern slope of the Lammermuir Hills and turned sharply north eastwards over an arch across Birns Water. After a final summit just short of 540ft, trains began an irregular descent down the Newhall Burn Valley past Bankrugg and Inglisfield to the secluded terminus amid woodland, about a third of a mile from the middle of Gifford, at around the 330ft mark.

Diminutive Drummond 4-4-0 tanks hauling elderly four wheel coaches at first, then demoted bogie stock later, provided the service for thirty years and trains worked through to Edinburgh Waverley.

Initially two departures each way took up to two hours for the journey of just 21 miles - an average of around 12mph! By World War I the timing was down to about 1 hour 10 minutes although this was still only about 18mph including some fast running on the main line. There were three workings each way, lunchtime extras on Saturdays, and even a late train on Saturday which arrived at Gifford just before midnight. For twenty years, prior to the ascendance of road transport, the railway was a boon to this rural area. The Gifford & Garvald remained nominally independent until absorbed by the LNER on 1st January 1923.

The demise of the Macmerry, Gullane and Gifford branches took place in fairly regular stages over a period of no less than 67 years, and both the first and last stretches of track to lose their traffic were part of the earliest routes to open. Through goods workings over the (in retrospect) unnecessary Smeaton to Hardengreen Junction line ceased as early as 1913 although the track remained in situ and various industrial sites continued to be served from either end. Another blatantly unsuccessful venture was the passenger service to Macmerry. The already meagre usage collapsed in the face of bus competition

Golfers predominated at Gullane station when this view was taken on 19th August 1914, although a young lad is sharing a joke with the stationmaster - distinguished by the white band around his cap - and a young lady is passing the time of day at the bookstall. The dog, as dogs have always done, showed little respect of Edwardian decorum. No less than five railway staff are visible illustrating the level of activity at even a small country terminus like this, eighty years ago. There was also an abundance of advertisements, including a large enamelled panel for Vim, and at the far end a large poster for the new North British Hotel in Edinburgh can be seen. Photograph W.F. Jackson, Glasgow University Archives.

Saltoun was a crossing point on the Gifford branch and actually boasted two platforms. Just prior to the grouping of 1923, North British Drummond 4-4-0T No.1467 stood at the station with a train for Edinburgh Waverley as the balancing eastbound service rolled in carrying the photographer. These rather quaint little engines which worked the line for most of its life were powerful enough to haul five coaches up the 1 in 50 gradients but still treated the lightweight track and structures kindly. The remaining examples were classified D51 by the LNER. The modest goods yard, consisting of two sidings and a loading bank with a crane, can be seen in the background, although traffic on this occasion consisted of just two wagons of hay covered by tarpaulins. A more amenable cargo was the fine malt whisky produced by Glenkinchie Distillery at Pencaitland just down the line. This can still be enjoyed in Edinburgh bars, but the last time it was despatched by rail was more than a quarter of a century ago. Photograph J.J. Cunningham.

Gullane station occupied a large tract of land at the south eastern corner of the village, almost 100ft up on the sandhills. In addition to the passenger platform there was a small engine shed, a loading bank and three sidings. Gullane was always a popular venue for Sunday School picnics and these continued after the end of regular services. In pre-war days the Glasgow Schools Necessitous Holiday Camps also contributed traffic; on one occasion two coaches were detached from a Glasgow High Street to Dunbar train and worked forward by the Gullane branch goods engine. On another occasion a Sunday School Special ran from Granton (one closed terminus to another - almost a pre-war rail tour!) taking a respectable 50 minutes despite 10mph and 20mph restrictions at the extremities of the journey. In bright sunshine at the end of a lovely day out, V3 2-6-2T No.67624 prepared to leave Gullane with a return Sunday School special on 21st June 1958. Evidence of the platform at Gullane could still be found amid wasteland between Victorian villas and a council estate in 1994, although there were proposals to build houses on the site. The flamboyant Marine Hotel on the extreme left is now a Fire Brigade training centre. Photograph W.S. Sellar.

to the extent that an average of just over one customer per train used the terminus when Macmerry and Winton stations closed on 1st July 1925. Remote Smeaton succumbed on 22nd September 1930 and golfers were denied the use of Luffness Platform from 1st June 1931. Passenger facilities were withdrawn from the Gullane branch itself on 12th September 1932, through portions of the 'Lothian Coast Express' having ceased ten years earlier. Services to Gifford were the next to go - on 3rd April 1933 - and that meant the end of Ormiston as well. The moribund Smeaton - Hardengreen Junction line was officially deleted from the map in 1934, apart from stubs at either end. After ten years of retrenchment there was a respite until Nature intervened, on 12th August 1948, when the Gifford branch was seriously breached at Humbie by torrential floodwater - though the terminus was served by road from Haddington until 1st May 1959. Goods traffic ceased at Macmerry and Winton on 2nd May 1960 and the Gifford branch was cut back further to Saltoun at the same time. Pencaitland yard finished on 23rd March 1964 and 25th May 1965 saw the end of goods traffic at Saltoun, Ormiston and Smeaton. Finally, when Dalkeith Washery closed in 1980 the rails from Monktonhall Junction became redundant and with the notable exception of North Berwick, the eastern branches were no more.

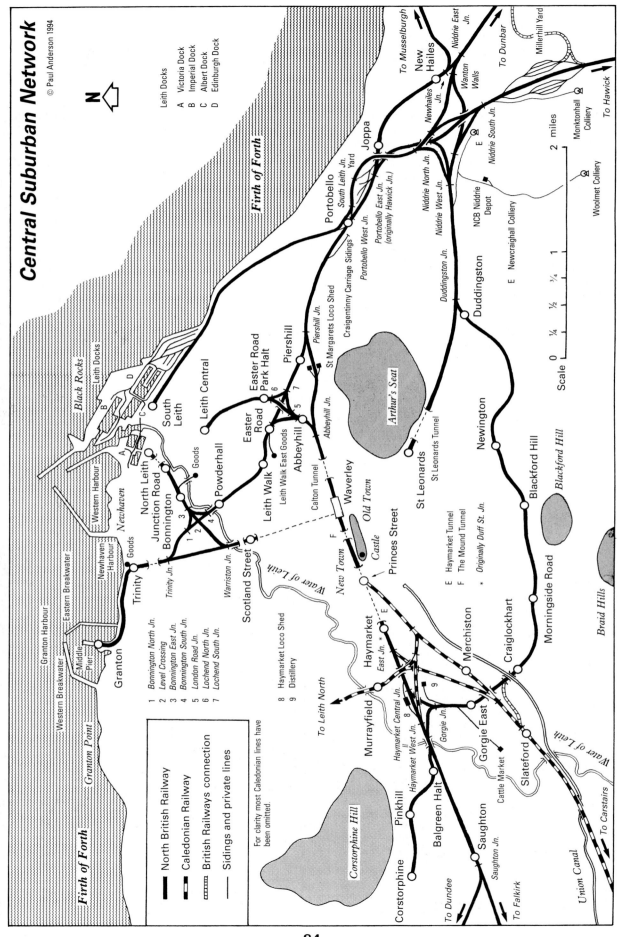

Central Suburban Network

© Paul Anderson 1994

N

Leith Docks
A Victoria Dock
B Imperial Dock
C Albert Dock
D Edinburgh Dock

1 Bonnington North Jn.
2 Level Crossing
3 Bonnington East Jn.
4 London Road Jn.
5 Lochend North Jn.
6 Lochend South Jn.
7
8 Haymarket Loco Shed
9 Distillery

E Haymarket Tunnel
F The Mound Tunnel
* Originally Duff St. Jn.

For clarity most Caledonian lines have been omitted.

━━━ North British Railway
▦▦▦ Caledonian Railway
▬▬▬ British Railways connection
──── Sidings and private lines

Scale
0   ¼   ½   ¾   1   2 miles

Chapter Six
Central Suburban

During the last quarter of the 19th century Edinburgh expanded considerably to the south and west of the Old Town. At the same time, streets of tenements were filling many of the gaps between the New Town and Leith. As a consequence the North British made several moves to enhance passenger facilities in the area and opened thirteen local stations around the city from 1884 to 1903, eleven of them within a two and a quarter mile radius of Waverley. This involved the construction of three new lines, although through goods traffic was a major consideration in one case. The existing branch from Piershill and Abbeyhill to Trinity and Bonnington gained four new stations. It was built primarily to improve access to Leith and Granton docks as described earlier, but eventually became a very useful link for north side communities. A more adventurous undertaking was a loop on the south side from Haymarket to Portobello, which incorpo-

rated part of the Edinburgh & Dalkeith alignment to St. Leonards. The main aim was to provide a freight bypass for Waverley, although the passenger business soon began to flourish as well. Two short suburban branches were built simultaneously during early Edwardian years, although in terms of architecture they were worlds apart. The first was a modest but handy line to the expanding village of Corstorphine three and a half miles west of the city centre and the scale of its stations was in keeping with the nearby villas. The second provided a long awaited direct route from the centre of Leith to the centre of Edinburgh and its breathtaking terminus was one of the most impressive suburban railway buildings in the whole of Britain.

NORTH SIDE IMPROVEMENTS AND SOUTH SIDE LOOP

In The Pioneers chapter earlier, the original purpose of the Piershill - Trinity line was outlined, but a brief recap may be

useful. It will be recalled that the first route from Waverley to Leith Docks and the Granton ferries was via the inconvenient cable worked incline through Scotland Street tunnel. Shortly after the North British inherited the former Edinburgh, Leith & Granton Railway in 1862, it set about building the deviation so that locomotive operation was possible throughout and mineral traffic had direct access from the Lothian coalfield and East Coast main line. The tracks began to carry goods on 2nd March 1868 and passenger services from Waverley to Leith and Granton via the spurs at Abbeyhill and Bonnington commenced three weeks later on 22nd March 1868. From Piershill Junction, about 100ft above sea level, the new route headed vaguely westwards past Restalrig and Lochend before passing under Easter Road and Leith Walk. Here it turned towards the north west and ran through Pilrig before dropping below 50ft to cross Water of Leith near Bonnington. After a level crossing with the original

On 21st August 1964 a Gloucester twin forming the 2.12pm from Musselburgh to Edinburgh Waverley called at Abbeyhill, having taken the loop from Piershill Junction. This view looking north towards London Road clearly shows the street level booking office, covered stairways and cream brick platform buildings dating from 1869. These featured timber frontages, shallow gabled roofs with plain bargeboards, squat chimneys and generous canopies. Far more interesting from the architectural point of view is Cadzow Place in the background. This very elegant tenement block had a wealth of dormer windows, chimneys and turrets - all of them different - and is worthy of close scrutiny. Somewhat moribund, Abbeyhill closed three weeks later when the Musselburgh service was withdrawn, but in its heyday the station was extremely busy. There were more than a hundred trains a day to Waverley in 1914, although by 1948 there were less than forty.

By the time Piershill station opened in 1891 the North British had adopted several standard elements for its smaller buildings and some of these were evident on 15th October 1960 as V1 2-6-2T No.67659 called with the 12.06pm from Edinburgh Waverley to Dunbar. In this instance poor quality red brick was the main material and windows were rectangular and rather uninspiring. The slate roofs had a fairly steep pitch and although the gable ends still displayed plain bargeboards they were enlivened by cross struts and delicate finials. Platform canopies were somewhat stunted, yet passengers were treated to glazed wind screens. Even the plain brick chimneys had fairly thoughtful stone cappings. The covered stairway on the left led down to Restalrig Road. From this angle Piershill station appears to be quite rural, but the houses of Marionville Avenue were away to the right and a large distillery off Dalgety Road peers through the mist in the distance. The five coach train is a bit of a concoction, consisting of Gresley and Thompson corridor and suburban stock plus a BR standard main line vehicle second from the rear. Piershill closed, along with Abbeyhill, on 7th September 1964.

Scotland Street - Leith line, the railway entered a curved cutting bridged by Ferry Road, then turned north to join the Scotland Street - Granton alignment near the southern portal of Trinity tunnel. The spur from Abbeyhill Junction to Easter Road, which brought in passenger trains from Waverley, was a broad sweeping curve through almost 180 degrees and it passed beneath London Road on the way.

At first the new line only had one intermediate station. This was situated on the east side of Leith Walk, a mile and three quarters from Waverley by train but less than half that by a stroll along the Walk itself. A long plain building associated with the railway still survives on the overbridge. However, the development of

Easter Road station had been closed for over thirteen years when this view, looking west, was taken on 15th October 1960. The North British did quite well to squeeze the booking office, stairways, platforms and waiting rooms into what was already, by 1891, a congested site. One peculiar outcome was the lofty chimneys on the up side building. The adjacent tenements were in a street called Sunnyside, although when an easterly breeze came off the Firth of Forth and the hearths had been stoked up, no doubt some residents questioned the validity of the name! Other tenements, in Elliot Street, can be seen bordering the track in the background. The signals controlled junctions at either end of the station. In the foreground the Piershill and Abbeyhill lines diverged whilst opposite the signal box, just beyond Easter Road bridge, a spur went off to Leith Walk East goods yard. Prior to the opening of Easter Road Park Halt on the Leith Central branch in 1950, this station was a popular way of reaching the Hibs ground.

Powderhall closed at the end of 1916 as a wartime economy measure, along with several other Edinburgh suburban stations, but this particular one never reopened. Seen here on 15th October 1960, the platform buildings were still in remarkably good condition. Apart from detail differences, these 1895 structures were virtually identical to those at Piershill and Easter Road. Broughton Road overbridge was behind the camera whilst in the background the track dips down to a bridge over Leith Water, to rise thence past the woodland of St. Marks Park, where the line to Bonnington and North Leith diverged.

the north side system soon began - albeit in a gentle way - with the opening of passenger facilities adjacent to London Road in Abbeyhill on 1st May 1869. The buildings set the general standard for many North British suburban stations in Edinburgh over subsequent decades by having a booking office at street level supplemented by substantial waiting rooms and offices on low level side platforms. A short but useful spur between Abbeyhill and Lochend Junction on the Trinity - Piershill line was authorised on 22nd July 1885 and opened on 1st October 1886. In effect it formed a minor loop of the main East Coast route, thus enabling Musselburgh and Dunbar locals to call at Abbeyhill. The mushrooming streets and tenements north east of the city centre were further served by stations at Piershill and Easter Road which opened

It was a warm summer evening when the 6.10pm from Waverley to Duddingston took the Edinburgh Suburban and Southside route at Haymarket Central Junction on 16th July 1962. Dieselisation was well advanced by this time and behind the Gloucester twin an English Electric Type 1 can be seen on Haymarket depot. A general decline anticipating the Beeching Report had already set in, and local services over the Circle ceased two months later. A train bound for Saughton Junction and the Forth Bridge was signalled on the main line.

Gorgie East (just Gorgie until May 1952) was the first station on the Inner Circle and had substantial buildings on each platform, reached by long ramps from Slateford Road. On 2nd February 1957 pristine B1 4-6-0 No.61117 of Parkhead shed arrived with the 11.51am football special from Partick Hill on the Glasgow Suburban network. This was a day of exceptionally heavy traffic, as in addition to the Hearts game at Tynecastle there was a rugby international at Murrayfield, generating no less than nine specials to Gorgie East alone. Murrayfield station dealt with ten trains and Dalry Road shed was overflowing with unfamiliar ex-LMS 4-6-0s including Jubilees Nos.45569 TASMANIA (Holbeck), 45600 BERMUDA (Patricroft), 45625 SARAWAK (Crewe North), 45672 ANSON (Camden) and 45689 AJAX (Longsight) from overnight Welsh specials. Slateford carriage sidings were crammed with empty stock, mainly ex-Great Western, and a rake of sleeping cars heated by No.55202 was provided at Lothian Road for railway staff. At Waverley (where proceedings during the morning had been enlivened by a special from Hawick hitting the buffer stops) twenty trains returned to Scottish stations, one headed for King's Cross, whilst three others left for Treherbert and Swansea Victoria in the early hours. Back at Gorgie East the distillery buildings off Robertson Avenue in the background still exist, although the station itself has been obliterated.

their doors on 1st May and 1st December 1891 respectively. Piershill was just off the main line and provided another incentive for stopping services to use the Abbeyhill loop. Finally, on 22nd April 1895 Powderhall station opened, in a somewhat quiet spot to the west of Broughton Road. Unfortunately, the expected housing developments did not materialise, so this particular passenger facility had a short and unremunerative life. However, for over twenty years the two miles of track from Piershill and Abbeyhill to Powderhall boasted five stations, an average of one every 700 yards.

The suburban line serving the south side of Edinburgh was largely custom built. It was also legally independent, although the North British was always behind the scheme. Acts of Parliament relevant to the Edinburgh Suburban & Southside Junction Railway were passed on 26th August 1880 and 24th July 1882 and progress with the almost continuous succession of earthworks was impressive. Goods traffic began on 31st October 1884 and passenger services followed on 1st December 1884, with the North British providing locomotives and rolling stock from the outset and absorbing the company completely on 1st May 1885. The 'Sub' began at westward and eastward facing junctions with the Edinburgh and

Glasgow main line, at Haymarket West and Haymarket Central Junctions respectively. These two spurs rose steadily on curved embankments and converged just north of a bridge over Gorgie Road. At Gorgie station (three quarters of a mile from Haymarket Central Junction) the line veered south eastwards and climbed at 1 in 80 through a half mile cutting spanned by no less than five bridges, carrying Slateford Road, the Caledonian

Haymarket branch, the Princes Street main line, the Union Canal and Colinton Road, in that order. After Craiglockhart station (mile and a quarter) the track entered a severe rock cutting which required brick buttresses to support the crumbling strata and a pumping engine to prevent flooding. A hefty stone arch carried Myreside Road across the railway, then the excavations became markedly shallower as far as the summit just west

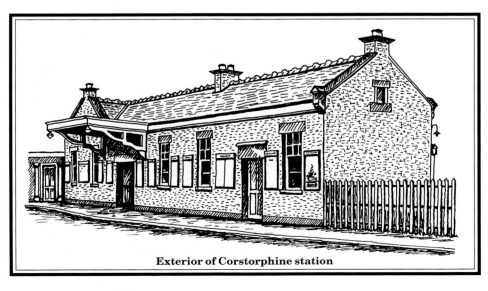

Exterior of Corstorphine station

The deep cutting between Gorgie and Craiglockhart had to be substantially modified when BR built the connection from Slateford on the former Caledonian main line during 1960. Seen from the Union Canal aqueduct, a Gloucester diesel multiple unit forming the 4.58pm from Musselburgh to Waverley via the Inner Circle, droned up the gradient from Gorgie East on 16th July 1962. Houses on Ashley Drive and Alderbank Gardens to the right, and a factory off Slateford Road to the left, formed the skyline. Two Caledonian bridges spanned the cutting in the distance, but the rather flimsy structures nearer the camera carried a water main. Note the sand drag and stop block protecting the junction.

Craiglockhart station opened on 1st June 1887, two and a half years after the Edinburgh Suburban and Southside passenger service began. It was out in the fields at first and actually closed from 1st May 1890 to 1st January 1891. Eventually several streets of villas developed around the railway, but passenger facilities were withdrawn again from 1st January 1917 to 1st February 1919, in the interests of wartime austerity. On 14th December 1957 St. Margarets D30 4-4-0 No.62421 LAIRD O' MONKBARNS rolled into Craiglockhart with the 12.39pm Inner Suburban train from Edinburgh Waverley. At this point the line was in a deep cutting, which had to be cut back and supported by retaining walls to accommodate the platforms.

of Morningside Road station (two miles). Continuing eastwards, the line descended at 1 in 85 through a sinuous cutting spanned by limestone bridges taking Braid Avenue, Oswald Road and Blackford Avenue across the formation.

A leafy suburb of opulent Edwardian villas grew up here and it was served by Blackford Hill station, just under three miles from Haymarket Central Junction. A sharper fall at 1 in 75, occasionally between stone retaining walls, brought the

route to Newington station (three and a half miles) which was between Mayfield Road and Mayfield Gardens. At last the line reverted to an elevated course on a long curved embankment past Cameron Toll and this afforded fine views of

Overcoats were the order of the day on 14th December 1957 as V1 2-6-2T No.67608 eased into Morningside Road with the 12.10pm Outer Circle working from Edinburgh Waverley, in bitter misty weather. The station, which was simply Morningside until October 1886, stood at the junction of Morningside Road, Cluny Gardens, Braid Road, Comiston Road and Balcarres Street and was surrounded by dwellings, making it the busiest on the 'Sub'. Posters on the station proclaimed 'The diesels are coming' and most Edinburgh local workings were taken over by Gloucester railcars during 1958. Back in the 1880s, Morningside Road had a 'what the butler saw' peep show machine on the platform, no doubt entertaining a few businessmen on their way to the city - but also generating letters of complaint to the North British Headquarters!

On 16th July 1962 a Gloucester twin forming the 4.34pm from Musselburgh to Waverley via the Inner Circle drew into Morningside Road to collect half a dozen passengers bound for the city. Stations on the Suburban and Southside line were generously proportioned and most of them had large brick platform buildings with hipped roofs, squat chimneys and big canopies, with their own sloping roofs springing somewhat unusually from the main structure. None of them survive, although the street level booking office at Morningside Road (which was of a similar design) still exists and has been converted into shops. The attractive North British footbridge is also in situ as it maintains a right of way between Balcarres Street and Maxwell Street. A fair sized goods yard, which can be seen in the background, outlived the passenger service by nearly five and a half years.

Arthur's Seat and the Old Town. Immediately east of Duddingston station the 'Sub' joined the old Edinburgh & Dalkeith branch to St. Leonards and passenger trains continued to Niddrie West Junction, Niddrie North Junction and Portobello. The line had climbed from about 150ft at Haymarket Junction to over 250ft at Morningside, but had dropped below 150ft again by Duddingston.

'Edinburgh Suburban & Southside Junction' was a very good description of the new line. The latter part of its name revealed the pressing need for a separate freight artery which would avoid the congestion at Waverley and provide an easy passage from the network north and west of Edinburgh to the Waverley route and East Coast main line. As predicted, traffic soon built up and by the early 1900s the 'Sub' was busy for 24 hours a day.

Although speed was in their favour, trains from most Southside Suburban stations had to pursue a roundabout course before reaching Waverley or Leith and this gave the trams a distinct advantage. On 16th November 1956 car No.50 waited at Braids terminus on Comiston Road, the journey taking it across nearly six miles of the city past Morningside Road station to Bruntsfield Place, Tollcross, Earl Grey Street, Lothian Road and Princes Street. After serving Waverley station, the route continued along Leith Walk, Pilrig Street and Newhaven Road to Stanley Road near the shore. Braids is an attractive area of spacious late Victorian houses. Braid Hills Road rises behind the car towards the 682ft volcanic summit whilst out of sight on the left trees masked the little Braid Burn as it tumbled down below 350ft. This was the last day of tram services, the 1936 extension to Fairmilehead having closed two months previously.

Newington station stood in a shallow cutting, with stone retaining walls, between Mayfield Road and Mayfield Gardens. Although this has long been a heavily built up area, the railway was bordered by trees, giving a deceptively rural appearance. Another unusual feature was the island platform, the only one on the line. On 19th November 1955 V3 2-6-2T No.67606 steamed into Newington with the 1.11pm Outer Circle service from Edinburgh Waverley.

Newington station was vulnerable to competition from tram routes 7 and 17 which reached out to the eastern flanks of the Braid Hills at Liberton. The journey to town passed a ribbon of houses along Craigmillar Park and Mayfield Gardens as far as the railway, but over the next mile and a half the service penetrated one of Edinburgh's most heavily populated inner suburbs. Minto Street, Newington Road, Clerk Street and Nicholson Street - each of them forming part of the main road from North Bridge to Penicuik and Peebles - yielded masses of passengers denied to the railway. The trams continued along Leith Walk and Pilrig Street to Stanley Road in Newhaven. On 19th November 1955 car No.256 whined up Liberton Brae, one of the steepest inclines on the Edinburgh system, as it climbed out of the Braid Burn Valley. Edwardian villas formed the backdrop but the terminus, a short distance away, was surrounded by 1920s semis. The Liberton tram service ended on 11th March 1956.

Overnight Aberdeen and West Highland 'fast fish' disturbed Morningside in the small hours and heavy coal trains from Fife and West Lothian pounded up the gradients with elderly 0-6-0s providing banking assistance. Long distance passenger workings ranged from royal specials bound for Deeside to summer excursions carrying English holidaymakers to the Highlands. Trip workings between Portobello and Haymarket served local goods yards, although Craiglockhart and Newington had no such facilities. When built, much of the line ran through open countryside, but the relentless march of suburbia pleased the North British board. As new housing developments took shape the hourly circular service in each direction began to fill up and when Waverley was rebuilt the south side suburban trains were given their own island platform. However, the true circular arrangement was soon broken with the opening of Leith Central which became the natural terminus at the eastern end, connections to and from Waverley being provided at Portobello. Because of its demanding gradients, the 'Sub' was largely worked by 0-4-2 tender locos at first, rather than the diminutive 4-4-0 tanks employed elsewhere on Edinburgh suburban duties. Eventually new 4-4-2Ts took over and these in turn were replaced by the highly competent V1 2-6-2Ts in the 1930s.

The erosion of passenger services on the inner suburban lines began with the

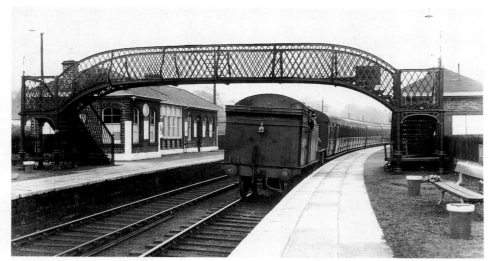

Duddingston station was on a fairly sharp curve where the suburban tracks veered eastwards to join the St. Leonards branch, the platforms standing less than a quarter mile from the junction. Access was from Duddingston Road West, but the village itself was more than half a mile away to the north in the shadow of Arthur's Seat, and some time elapsed before nearby Craigmillar developed as a housing area. However a particularly pure and prolific supply of spring water had led to the establishment of several breweries close to the route of the railway and for many years these depended on the trains to bring in workers. Framed by another fine North British footbridge, V3 2-6-2T No.67609 stood at Duddingston with the 2.05pm Outer Circle working to Edinburgh Waverley on 21st May 1955. Further details of the rather confident architectural style adopted by the Southside line may be gleaned from this view. The proud building on the far platform, which incorporated the booking office, featured fashionable 'School Board' windows below segmental arches, a prominent clock, timber screening for the waiting room frontage, and deep guttering giving a very solid edge to the roof.

Shortly after it was formed, British Railways began to sort out the confusion brought about by similarly named facilities, so the ex-LNER goods depot on Leith Walk gained the suffix East in April 1952 whilst Gorgie passenger station and goods yard on the circle became Gorgie East during May 1952. A positive move was the opening of a double track link between Slateford and Craiglockhart in 1960.

This allowed freight transfers between the former Caledonian and North British systems in the Edinburgh area, a function which had previously been carried out by the single line across Granton Square. Retrenchment resumed with the end of passenger services over the Suburban & Southside Junction on 10th September 1962 and continued with the closure of Piershill and Abbeyhill stations on 7th September 1964. The pick up goods ceased to shunt Gorgie East, Morningside Road and Duddingston on 5th February 1968, although the first and last remained open for private industrial customers for a while. Bonnington depot finished on 22nd July 1968 but occasional traffic from Granton gasworks continued to use the track through Trinity and Easter Road until 1986. The north side line is still open from Piershill to the Edinburgh refuse loading point at Powderhall and through freight still uses the 'Sub'. For several years there has been talk of reinstating passenger services over the latter.

closure of lightly used Powderhall, Leith Walk and Craiglockhart on 1st January 1917 to release staff for other wartime duties. Powderhall never reopened but the other two appeared in the timetable again from 1st February 1919. Tramway competition finally finished off Leith Walk on 31st March 1930, and Easter Road closed on 16th June 1947 when the North Leith to Waverley service was withdrawn.

CORSTORPHINE AND LEITH CENTRAL

Although now making up one of Edin-

Portobello enjoyed a much enhanced timetable following the inauguration of Southside services and was rebuilt shortly afterwards. When most suburban workings via Duddingston were diverted to and from Leith Central it adopted the role of an interchange for Waverley passengers. On 14th December 1957 the 1.11pm Outer Circle working from Edinburgh paused with Stanier 2-6-2T No.40159 in charge; three of these unpopular engines had been transferred to St. Margarets shed for local duties the previous summer. J38 0-6-0 No.65927 waited to leave the adjacent yard with a freight and a couple of V2 2-6-2s ambled past, completing a busy scene.

burgh's largest suburbs, Corstorphine was originally a small farming village in the shadow of Corstorpine Hill. It grew up around a 14th century castle and was separated from the city by a marsh and loch stretching away towards Water of Leith. The medieval kirk has an unusual square tower which once had a beacon to guide worshippers across the mire, and this strange feature is still commemorated by a symbolic electric light. There was also a sulphurous spring which elevated the village to the status of a minor spa during the early 1800s. From 1842 Corstorphine had a station on the Edinburgh & Glasgow Railway, but this was three quarters of a mile away to the south and hardly more convenient than slow horse-drawn conveyances along the main road through Murrayfield. Sixty years later the little settlement acquired its own railway, although the North British was just as concerned about blocking Caledonian aspirations for an extension from Barnton to Dalry as serving the district more effectively. An Act for the line from Haymarket West Junction to Corstorphine was obtained on 12th August 1898 and the branch, a mile and a quarter of double track, opened on 1st February 1902. It ran parallel to the main line for a quarter of a mile, veering away northwards beyond a bridge over Balgreen Road to continue on an embankment which later became sandwiched between Saughtonhall estate and the Carrick Knowe Golf Course. A westerly course was resumed at a bridge over The Stank, and Pinkhill station (three quarters of a mile from Haymarket West) stood just beyond here on an overbridge. Several acres of land between roads called Paddockholm and Traquair Park West were acquired for the terminus just east of the village centre. Despite being dominated by the slopes of Corstorphine Hill, the line was easily graded and kept to the 150ft contour for much of its length, merely dipping slightly to cross The Stank. A fairly intensive service was provided. In summer 1914 for instance there were 24 trains each way from about 7.00am to 11.00pm and the occasional long distance working to places as far away as Berwick upon Tweed appeared during the 1920s.

By the late 1880s Leith had three well established passenger services to Edinburgh, although none of them were particularly direct and that from South Leith involved changing trains at Portobello. Furthermore, their respective termini were down by the docks rather than in the town centre. Rumblings of a new Caledonian suburban line serving much of Leith sounded alarm bells in North British headquarters and at the end of 1889 the company began to formulate plans for a direct route from Waverley to the foot of Leith Walk. A lengthy incubation period followed, but eventually the mile long

Corstorphine station and its associated yards occupied a huge tract of land on the eastern edge of the village. Its two side platforms were very wide, and long enough to accommodate a twelve coach train, yet they possessed neither canopies nor shelters. No doubt the waiting room in the concourse building was deemed adequate for passengers during inclement weather. On 7th September 1954 D34 4-4-0 No.62487 GLEN ARKLET brought the 6.15pm from Edinburgh Waverley gently over the engine release scissors crossing towards the buffer stops at Corstorphine. The six coach train consisted of Gresley, Thompson and BR Standard corridor coaches in 'blood and custard' livery. Such luxury was commonplace on local workings at the time, as the station was used to stable main line stock between express duties, and part-rakes were frequently employed on the short journey to the city. The carriage sidings are on the right, whilst the goods yard is off to the left.

A couple of non-gangwayed suburban coaches and four Gresley main line vehicles formed the 6.17pm from Corstorphine to Edinburgh Waverley on 7th September 1954. V1 2-6-2T No.67670 was in charge. This view towards the concourse at Corstorphine shows the station building across the end of the tracks. It was a straightforward red brick structure forming a reverse L shape in plan, but by 1902 the growing Edwardian tendency for grand architectural gestures had begun to influence the North British, even when it was designing lesser stations. Although merely single storey, the building was remarkably lofty and had a big gabled roof finished off with prominent crested ridge tiles. The windows were plain yet tall, and there was a canopy on the platform side mirrored by a bold porch hood over the street entrance. A sandstone parapet hid the eaves and the gable ends were projected upwards, and corbelled outwards recalling the much earlier Peebles Railway style. As a crowning touch, pronounced capping stones gave the chimneys a very distinctive appearance. Unfortunately this particular example of late North British architecture has been demolished.

double track branch was built, somewhat unusually without its own Act of Parliament, and opened for passenger traffic on 1st July 1903. It began at London Road Junction on the Abbeyhill - Piershill spur, then crossed the Easter Road - Piershill line before curving through a substantial cutting and dropping down a 1 in 62 incline parallel to Lochend Road. A spur was provided at Lochend so that suburban trains from the Southside circle had direct access. In Leith itself a large amount of land was acquired and numerous tenements together with several commercial premises were demolished. Even the street pattern was altered. Leith Central occupied a whole block bounded by Leith Walk, Duke Street, Easter Road and Gordon Street, and although the huge terminus was already above street level it was given a soaring overall roof which dominated much of the surrounding area. The sheer size of the place caused surprise at the time of construction and has attracted comments ever since. It seems

that the North British was following the Caledonian's penchant for grand buildings and indeed, from the approach tracks, there was a distinct resemblance to Princes Street station. However, compared with all this magnificence at rail level, the facade on Leith Walk was quite restrained. Despite its over-capacity the station was busy at first and there were no less than 54 weekday departures in the summer of 1914. Most workings were of a purely local nature, namely the 'Penny Jerks' to and from Waverley and the Inner and Outer Circle trains, but there were some longer distance services to Glasgow Hyndland and Dundee Tay Bridge.

Leith Central began to decline in the 1920s after the Edinburgh tramways were electrified and through journeys from the town centre to Princes Street became possible. Buses were the main threat to loadings on the Corstorphine branch, but a counter attack was the opening of Balgreen Halt during 1934 -

an attempt to attract traffic from the Saughtonhall area. The Leith branch also gained a new station in 1950, but Easter Road Park Halt was specifically built to bring visiting football fans to the adjacent Hibernian FC stadium. However, the ordinary passenger service was on its last legs by this time and the end came on 7th April 1952. Although there was no goods traffic, the massive terminus survived as a carriage depot - an additional function which it had in fact performed from the outset. In 1957 it became Edinburgh's main diesel multiple unit stabling point. Despite an eruption of protests, the Corstorphine branch passenger service was withdrawn on 1st January 1968 and with the closure of Corstorphine goods yard on 5th February 1968 the line was abandoned. Leith Central diesel depot closed during 1972 and the giant train shed stood idle while its future was debated. It was demolished in 1989.

The 11.10am from Corstorphine to North Berwick on 14th December 1957, consisting of three non-corridor coaches hauled by V3 2-6-2T No.67617, was a much more conventional suburban train than many of those on the branch. It is seen entering Pinkhill station where signs advised passengers to alight for the Zoological Park. Edinburgh Zoo was established on 70 acres of nearby Corstorphine Hill in 1913 and eventually became famous for its collection of penguins, which entertained visitors with their daily parade around the grounds. The main building at Pinkhill was of a similar style to that at Corstorphine, although its perch on the wide girder span required the use of lightweight wooden frames and panels. It was complemented by a pleasant little pavilion on the up platform consisting of a mixture of brick and timber. The bridge connected Corstorphine Road, behind the trees on the right, with a steeply sloping driveway, simply called Pinkhill.

Most of Leith Central stood on a huge plinth, its rubble-faced walls enclosing a gloomy undercroft with commercial accommodation for rent. Hefty dressed stone walls treated with classical details both internally and externally rose above the plinth, providing support for the great roof which gave the station its character. In plan this was lozenge shaped, like Princes Street, and expanded from less than 100ft. at the throat to over 200ft. half way to the buffer stops. It also provided cover for virtually all 260 yards of the two island platforms. A series of deep lattice girders raked inwards at the edges, rested on the walls and provided support for thirteen transverse gables. These were fully glazed and rose to louvred smoke vents with their own little gables some 60ft. above rail level. The most beautiful feature of the train shed was a superb glass screen at the outer end, which had slender mullions exquisitely interrupted by a diamond pattern towards the top. On 19th April 1965 preserved Great North of Scotland Railway 4-4-0 No.49 GORDON HIGHLANDER rested outside Leith Central with the 'Scottish Rambler' Easter weekend tour. The train was straddling Easter Road on a plate girder bridge which was four tracks wide and had abutments faced in glazed white bricks to counter the gloom below. The break in the tenements is a clear indication of how the North British had to purchase and demolish property to reach Leith town centre. But the wheel has turned full circle and the gap is now filled with a modern four storey block.

After crossing the Piershill - Trinity line, the Leith Central branch entered a deep yet broad half mile cutting which first curved past Lochend Loch then straightened out below Lochend Road. During 1950 this unlikely site was used to accommodate Easter Road Park Halt, designed to cope with a huge influx of away supporters when Hibernian FC were playing at home. It only had a single platform for arrivals, and departures were from Abbeyhill. On 15th October 1960 Standard class 5 4-6-0 No.73122 made a punctual 1.55pm arrival with the 12.51pm football special from Glasgow Queen Street for a Hibs -v- Celtic fixture. This was followed by the 1.10pm departure from Queen Street which was also composed of non-corridor stock and had sister loco No.73108 in charge. The floodlights of Easter Road Park Stadium can be seen on the right. Lochend North Junction, where the spur from Piershill came in, is pinpointed by the signals above the train, whilst the Piershill - Trinity line itself ran from left to right between the factory in the middle distance and the distillery off Dalgety Road prominent on the skyline. Two bridges spanned the Leith Central branch behind the camera, one carrying Hawkhill Avenue and the other taking the Caledonian New Lines towards the shore.

Balgreen Halt opened on 29th January 1934, at the start of the curve where Corstorphine trains headed away from the main line, and in this view the routes to Glasgow and the Forth Bridge are prominent on the right. Access was from the junction of Balgreen Road and Saughtonhall Drive off to the left. Pleasant LNER buildings featuring tiled pyramidal roofs with large overhangs were provided, although the platforms and fencing were somewhat basic. This was the site of a temporary station erected in 1908 for the Scottish National Exhibition at nearby Saughton Park, which received a train every quarter of an hour at peak times. On 12th October 1957 Ivatt 2MT 2-6-0 No.46461 ran into Balgreen Halt with the 1.38pm from North Berwick to Corstorphine.

On 18th August 1963 V2 2-6-2 No.60882 rumbled through the North Queensferry tower, running wrong line because of work on the track, with the 2.40pm from Edinburgh Waverley to Cowdenbeath. The permanent way base of 28ft oak logs and the special flat bottomed rails can be seen in this view. 'Like painting the Forth Bridge' has long been a phrase used to describe an endless task, and there is more than a ring of truth about it. From 1883 some 45 painters worked continuously on the structure and took three years to progress from end to end. One coat used up almost 54 tons of paint! Nowadays a more sophisticated covering is employed and it lasts much longer, so the activity tends to be spasmodic.

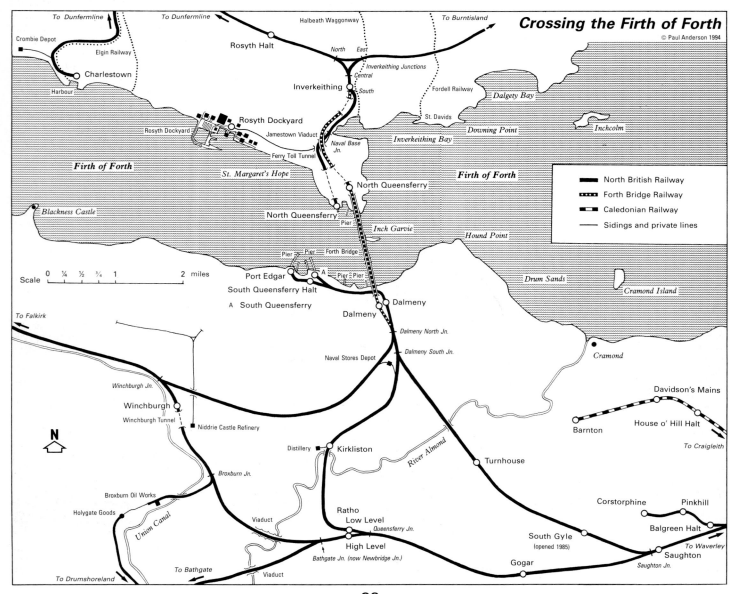

Crossing the Firth of Forth

© Paul Anderson 1994

Legend:
- North British Railway
- Forth Bridge Railway
- Caledonian Railway
- Sidings and private lines

Chapter Seven

Crossing the Firth of Forth

The Forth Bridge is still one of the engineering Wonders of the World, despite having been built over a century ago. Even today it is an awesome sight, particularly from North Queensferry where the mighty tangle of red oxide girders rears above the old stone cottages. On bright summer days it presents a colourful contrast to the blues and greens of the estuary, in an autumn mist it takes on an air of mystery and on bleak winter nights it becomes a black mass against the sky. The grandeur of the bridge can only really be appreciated from below, for a journey across it can be slightly disappointing. True, there is a fine view of the Firth, but for much of the time this is interrupted by girders, stout and slender, solid and latticed, at seemingly crazy angles. Careful study from a distance is necessary before trying to understand how the steelwork fits together when viewed from a train. Apart from tourists and enthusiasts, most people do not bother. Commuters on the Fife Circle tend to take the massive engineering work for granted and after a day

at work in Edinburgh, shop girls and young executives alike are more interested in a quick nap, a browse through the evening paper or planning the evening ahead than looking out of the carriage window. The sheer scale of the Forth Bridge reflects the importance of this estuary crossing which has been an essential feature of communications in eastern Scotland for nearly a thousand years. A ferry existed at Queensferry from the 11th century to the opening of the Forth Road bridge, whilst the pioneering railway boats from Granton to Burntisland replaced long established crossings, from Newhaven and Leith. Plans for a fixed link go back nearly three hundred years and some of them were highly fanciful. The construction and maintenance of the Forth Bridge itself include some mind boggling statistics and although these have been well documented they are well worth another airing.

GRANTON TO BURNTISLAND

The railway approach to this crossing and the early development of Granton Har-

bour were outlined in Chapter One, but a re-cap and further details are appropriate. Work on the ferry piers began in October 1837 and was completed during 1845, a modest passenger service from Victoria Jetty to Burntisland using sailing boats starting in 1838 in competition with the long established passage from Newhaven to Pettycur near Kinghorn. However, the journey in a small pinnace or yawl on either route was uncomfortable and could be terrifying in stormy weather. A substantial improvement was heralded by the Duke of Buccleuch's Burntisland & Granton Pier & Ferry Act of 1842 which stipulated that at least three steam boats must be employed on eight return crossings in summer and six in winter 'unless prevented by tempestuous weather'. This operation began on 15th September 1844, initially using sailing vessels, and by the following year some 400 people a day were making use of the various boats plying from Granton. The first steam boat, named FORTH, entered service during 1846 and in 1847 the Edinburgh & Northern Railway

Preserved Black 5 4-6-0 No.44871 SOVEREIGN crosses the Forth Bridge approach viaduct above North Queensferry with a Scottish Railway Preservation Society 'Santa Special' on 5th December 1992. The train used the surburban line from Waveley and thence the Fife Circle, making a second trip during the afternoon. These workings were repeated the following Saturday with A4 Pacific No. 60009 UNION OF SOUTH AFRICA. The view itself has altered very little since the bridge was built.

North British Railway Forth Passenger Ferry 'William Muir'

(Burntisland Pier & Ferry) Act transferred the Duke of Buccleuch's operations to railway ownership. Two more paddle steamers, AULD REEKIE and THANE OF FIFE, were introduced during 1847 and effectively wiped out any competition, including the old Newhaven - Pettycur sailings then operated by Fife & Lothian Ferries. Burntisland saw a massive upturn in its fortunes. The Romans had recognised its natural advantages as a port and Cromwell built new quays in the mid 1600s, but two centuries of stagnation had followed. With the construction of the Edinburgh - Granton Railway in 1842-47 and the Burntisland - Perth/Tayport system in 1847-50 the future of the five mile Granton - Burntisland passage was assured. Furthermore, increasing coal and iron exports from Fife made Burntisland a boom port.

The combined rail and water transect from Edinburgh to the north was acceptable enough for passengers, but it was proving inconvenient for goods traffic. A solution emerged in 1848 when local newspapers announced the construction of a 'floating railroad' for the Tay crossing. It took the form of a revolutionary 399 ton paddle steamer called LEVIA-THAN which was specially designed to carry 34 wagons on a through deck equipped with rails. Twin funnels rose from the sides rather than the centre line and a lofty bridge spanned the deck. The

Although the Granton - Burntisland passenger ferry was suspended by the LNER at the beginning of the war and officially abandoned in 1946, a new company started a vehicle carrying service in 1952. It employed four converted tank landing craft and one of them, GLENFINNAN (the others were BONNIE PRINCE CHARLIE, ERISKAY and FLORA MACDONALD), had just arrived at Granton on 26th May 1952, having carried half a dozen cars, two lorries and a Pickfords pantechnicon. The vessel is alongside the former passenger ferry ramp, not to be confused with the old train ferry berth which was on the shore. Beyond the ancient single deck bus and transit shed on the right, the canopy of Granton station can just be made out. The basic timber structure dealt with its last regular passenger trains some 27 years earlier. Granton - Burntisland operations were abandoned at the end of 1952 after the craft had been plagued with problems and they were eventually sold abroad. On 30th March 1991 Forth Ferries Ltd commenced operations with a catamaran named SPIRIT OF FIFE, having a passenger capacity of 250. It also offered cruises and there were bus connections to and from the city centre. This service also seems to have foundered.

Edinburgh Perth & Dundee decided to use its new vessel on the Granton - Burntisland link where it performed sterling service from 1849 to 1890. A duplicate steamer, the BALBIRNIE, was introduced in 1861 and KINLOCH and MIDLOTHIAN followed after the North British took over. With a 20ft tide in the Firth, loading and unloading wagons presented a problem. At first hydraulic cranes were used but eventually special slipways, wheeled cradles and cables worked by stationary steam engines pro-

Burntisland was an important link in the chain of communication from Edinburgh to the north before the Forth Bridge opened. In this October 1964 view of grimy B1 4-6-0 No.61343 clanking out of the town with an eastbound freight, the line down to the original terminus used by ferry passengers is on the left. The route from Inverkeithing to Burntisland, which the train had traversed, opened in 1890 and this new alignment incorporated through platforms adjacent to the old station. Burntisland Junction signal box on the right closed in 1936 when its duties were taken over by Burntisland East cabin, this in turn succumbing when the Edinburgh Signalling Centre opened during 1979.

FORTH BRIDGE NORTH (night shift) : OCTOBER 1952/3		
TRAIN	pass	DESTINATION
20.35 DUNDEE	22.08	EDINBURGH (22.24)
15.45 Heaton	22.11	Craiginches (02.50)
19.13 Cadder	22.21	Inverkeithing (22.32)
19.10 ABERDEEN	22.24	KINGS CROSS (07.15)
22.35 EDINBURGH	22.56	THORNTON JCN (23.51)
22.45 EDINBURGH	23.04	PERTH (00.26)
19.42 Dundee	23.14	Heaton (03.51)
21.00 Thornton Jcn	23.28	Cowlairs (02.55)
21.35 Niddrie	23.36	Stirling (03.25)
19.45 Forfar	23.37	South Leith (00.40)
23.10 EDINBURGH	23.26	PERTH (00.38)
22.05 Dundee	23.48	Carlisle (04.04)
21.40 Leith Walk	23.56	Dundee (02.32)
20.20 Aberdeen	23.58	Carlisle (05.19)
22.35 Niddrie	00.20	Craiginches (05.43)
22.20 Thornton Jcn	00.22	South Leith (01.25)
22.45 Cadder	00.33	Dundee (04.28)
00.30 Inverkeithing	00.39	Kings Cross (15.05)
00.42 Inverkeithing	00.42	Heaton (05.26)
22.26 Leith Walk	00.50	Perth (02.55)
00.55 Inverkeithing	01.04	Carlisle (05.26)
23.40 Leith Walk	01.09	Methil (03.45)
11.55 Burntisland	01.19	Portobello (02.10)
23.55 South Leith	01.30	Thornton Junction (03.05)
22.45 Perth	01.30	Portobello (02.33)
23.25 Cadder	01.41	Glencraig Jcn (03.20)
21.35 Stirling	01.48	Portobello (02.55)
00.10 Niddrie	01.54	Perth (07.30)
23.30 Thornton	01.59	Cadder (04.19)
23.15 Bo'ness	02.10	Townhill Jcn (03.02)
22.25 Aberdeen	02.18	Carlisle Upperby (09.10)
17.50 Carlisle	02.23	Craiginches (09.00)
23.05 Broughty Ferry	02.28	Carlisle (10.59)
22.50 Dundee	02.37	Cadder (04.40)
01.20 Niddrie	02.43	Dundee (05.30)
01.00 Thornton	02.52	Carlisle (11.37)
01.10 Bathgate	02.59	Burntisland (03.10)
23.45 Dundee	03.07	Portobello (04.30)
00.30 Cadder	03.09	Thornton Jcn (05.20)
00.15 Perth	03.22	South Leith (04.25)
00.50 Gunnie	03.24	Inverkeithing (03.34)
00.30 Dundee	03.37	Carlisle (12.14)
19.00 KINGS CROSS	03.46	ABERDEEN (06.55)
02.30 Dunfermile (EBV)	03.54	Cadder (05.49)
22.45 Aberdeen	04.06	Portobello (05.25)
02.32 Niddrie	04.14	Stirling (07.10)
23.05 Dundee	04.22	Niddrie (05.10)
02.15 Thornton Jcn	04.39	Portobello (05.46)
03.30 Niddrie	04.45	Burntisland (05.18)
00.05 Montrose	04.52	South Leith (06.20)
02.55 Cadder	04.55	Inverkeithing (05.05)
04.50 Inverkeithing	05.04	Gunnie (07.16)
04.00 Townhill Jcn	05.19	Polmont (06.02)
05.05 EDINBURGH	05.21	CRAIL (07.310)
01.10 Carlisle	05.41	Dundee (07.30)
00.20 Craiginches	05.42	Heaton (16.42)
01.30 Carlisle	05.56	Perth (07.20)
01.55 Perth	05.59	Meadows (07.23)

vided the transition from boat to shore. In 1876 an imposing new passenger paddle steamer called JOHN STIRLING replaced the venerable FORTH which became a coal barge before ending up as a rusting hulk on Granton beach. The equally impressive WILLIAM MUIR, capable of taking up to 950 passengers, entered service in 1879.

Just four years later the Forth Bridge began to take shape and a drastic change in the fortunes of the ferries was inevitable. Nevertheless the Granton crossing continued to perform a vital function, notably one fine autumn night in 1889 when George Sanger's Circus and Menagerie - comprising 50 caravans, 500 horses and all manner of animals - was shipped north between 10pm and 4am. The largest elephant, inevitably called 'Jumbo' helped tow caravans along the pier, although one of its younger companions made itself rather unpopular by snatching a loaf of bread, intended for railway workers, from the grasp of an inspector! When the bridge opened in 1890 all but one of the paddle steamers became redundant. The specialist freight boats found

The graceful suspension bridge in the background could well have been a ghost of the 1818 scheme for a stagecoach crossing, as ferries QUEEN MARGARET and ROBERT THE BRUCE went about their time honoured duties at Hawes Pier, South Queensferry, on 21st August 1964. In reality it was the Forth Road Bridge nearing completion. Two weeks later the fine structure, which both rivalled and complemented the original Forth Bridge, was opened for traffic and brought the Queensferry passage to an end.

no further use and were eventually broken up, but AULD REEKIE, THANE OF FIFE and JOHN STIRLING were sold for further service. WILLIAM MUIR soldiered on alone, carrying the 230 or so people a day who preferred the boat to the bridge. The vessel became a minesweeper at Sheerness while the service

FORTH BRIDGE NORTH (Early turn): OCTOBER 1952/3		
TRAIN	pass	DESTINATION
05.50 EDINBURGH	06.10	ROSYTH DOCKS (06.33)
04.25 Burntisland	06.12	Bathgate (07.52)
05.55 EDINBURGH	06.15	DUNDEE (08.19)
01.00 Craiginches	06.22	Carlisle (16.04)
06.08 EDINBURGH	06.29	STIRLING (07.37)
06.20 EDINBURGH	06.41	BURNTISLAND (07.05)
02.00 Stirling	06.49	Portobello (08.02)
06.28 EDINBURGH	06.50	PERTH (08.36)
06.40 EDINBURGH	06.56	DUNDEE (08.33)
06.40 DUNFERMLINE	07.05	EDINBURGH (07.27)
06.50 EDINBURGH	07.12	ROSYTH DOCKS (07.42)
07.05 Inverkeithing	07.19	Cadder (10.08)
06.31 LEVEN	07.44	EDINBURGH (08.06)
07.30 EDINBURGH	07.49	ABERDEEN (11.17)
07.40 EDINBURGH	07.59	PERTH (09.12)
06.25 PERTH	08.02	EDINBURGH (08.21)
07.50 EDINBURGH	08.11	STIRLING (09.16)
06.05 DUNDEE	08.11	EDINBURGH (08.33)
07.27 THORNTON JCN	08.22	EDINBURGH (08.41)
08.05 EDINBURGH	08.26	THORNTON JCN (09.19)
06.45 CRAIL	08.28	EDINBURGH (08.52)
07.41 THORNTON JCN	08.35	GLASGOW (09.47)
06.25 Cadder	08.36	Inverkeithing (08.46)
06.53 DUNDEE	08.50	EDINBURGH (09.11)
07.40 GLASGOW	08.53	THORNTON JCN (09.47)
08.45 EDINBURGH	09.06	PERTH (10.34)
07.55 STIRLING	09.08	EDINBURGH (09.30)
07.30 Polmont	09.16	Inverkeithing (09.26)
06.00 ABERDEEN	09.24	EDINBURGH (09.40)
09.10 EDINBURGH	09.29	DUNDEE (11.21)
08.18 PERTH	09.32	NEWCASTLE (10.25)
08.45 GLASGOW	09.56	DUNDEE via CRAIL (12.45)
09.45 Inverkeithing	09.59	Cadder (11.38)
05.00 Montrose	10.12	Carlisle (17.24)
10.00 EDINBURGH	10.16	ABERDEEN (13.34)
10.10 Inverkeithing	10.24	Polmont (11.40)
10.10 EDINBURGH	10.29	PERTH (11.47)
09.10 PERTH	10.35	EDINBURGH (10.54)
08.55 Niddrie	10.38	Dundee (13.25)
08.38 DUNDEE	10.44	EDINBURGH (11.03)
07.32 DUNDEE via CRAIL	10.54	GLASGOW (11.58)
10.40 EDINBURGH	11.01	DUNDEE via TAYPORT (13.37)
09.20 Niddrie	11.10	Townhill Jcn (11.36)
10.08 STIRLING	11.12	EDINBURGH (11.34)
08.55 ABERDEEN	11.26	EDINBURGH (11.48)
04.50 Aberdeen	11.37	South Leith (12.49)
10.25 Niddrie	11.38	Thornton Jcn (13.00)
10.57 THORNTON JCN	11.48	GLASGOW (12.54)
11.30 EDINBURGH	11.49	THORNTON JCN (12.42)
09.35 Perth	12.02	Portobello (13.00)
09.35 Broughty Ferry	12.22	South Leith (13.48)
04.05 Heaton	12.29	Craiginches (17.22)
11.10 Burntisland	12.35	Cadder (14.19)
12.35 Inverkeithing	12.49	Cadder (15.12)
11.40 LEVEN	12.58	EDINBURGH (13.18)
12.09 THORNTON JCN	13.04	EDINBURGH (13.26)
06.05 Carlisle	13.18	Craiginches (18.58)
09.55 ABERDEEN	13.21	EDINBURGH (13.37)
13.09 EDINBURGH	13.30	DUNDEE (15.25)
12.08 PERTH	13.31	EDINBURGH (13.50)
11.00 Perth	13.44	South Leith (15.03)
13.25 EDINBURGH	13.46	STIRLING (14.51)
12.51 GLASGOW	13.56	KIRKALDY (14.28)

Kirkliston was the principal intermediate station on the branch from Ratho to South Queensferry. It was built of red brick relieved by cream brick dressings, and had a hipped slate roof and timber fronted waiting room. When the Forth Bridge approaches from Saughton and Winchburgh opened, the branch became virtually superfluous apart from purely local needs. The village of Kirkliston was on the main Glasgow to Edinburgh road and looked to the latter rather than Queensferry. Consequently, the station was no match for bus services to the city despite its convenient site, so its demise in 1930 was hardly a surprise. This view was taken on 5th April 1959 when there was still residual coal traffic to the goods yard, together with distillery traffic.

was suspended from the beginning of 1917 to mid-1919. She was finally retired on 2nd March 1937 having made an estimated 80,000 crossings and was sadly dismantled. A replacement vessel (built for Wallasey Corporation's New Brighton - Liverpool service) kept the Granton crossing going until World War II but the second suspension because of hostilities proved the death knell for Edinburgh's railway ferries.

QUEENSFERRY

The Queensferry passage is one of the oldest estuary crossings in the world. Legend has it that the name was derived from Queen Margaret who settled in Dunfermline around 1068 and frequently visited Edinburgh. Her boat also provided a free crossing for pilgrims heading for St. Andrews. One of her sons, King David I - the founder of Holyrood and Melrose Abbeys - placed the ferry under the custody of the abbots of Dunfermline who ap-

The ascent from South Queensferry to Dalmeny was quite severe and J36 0-6-0 No.65258 was making a determined effort with the return South Queensferry goods on 15th August 1961 as it passed beneath an occupation bridge, within sight of Dalmeny station on the Forth Bridge line. This stretch of trackbed is now a footpath.

4,300 carts, 13,000 horses and 43,000 sheep and cattle were handled. The first steamer, appropriately named QUEEN MARGARET entered service during 1821 and just over twenty years later the last sailing vessel retired.

In 1845 the Edinburgh & Glasgow Railway began to show interest in the passage and promoted a line from Ratho to South Queensferry, but nothing was

A halt was eventually built between Dunfermline and Inverkeithing on the original approach to North Queensferry. It served new housing known as the 'Garden City', associated with the rapid development of Rosyth Dockyard following the outbreak of World War I. Although the platforms were fairly lengthy, economy seems to have been the watchword elsewhere. Very basic wooden shelters were provided and the lamp posts were pieces of old rail. The booking office facing Queensferry Road was carried on stilts and the rudimentary station was served by an extension of the Dunfermline & District Tramways Company, at the request of the Admiralty. By early LNER days the halt was appearing in the public timetable, probably in an attempt to increase traffic following the post-war rundown of the naval base. On 27th February 1960 B1 4-6-0 No.61245 MURRAY OF ELIBANK arrived at Rosyth Halt with the 12.15pm from Edinburgh Waverley to Cardenden, formed of a finely turned out set of Gresley corridor coaches. The station still serves the sprawl of houses stretching away to the right.

pointed the boatmen and took a quarter of the revenue. In 1275 boatmen selected by the fathers were given a monopoly and only their heirs could take over the crossing rights. Over the centuries parliament made several attempts to change these hereditary arrangements, but it was not until 1809 that a body of trustees was incorporated to work the ferries. Despite

the use of small sailing boats, the Queensferry passage was extremely lucrative by this time. Income was as much as £5,000 per annum and up to 450 people made the crossing on busy days, although charges were waived for 'carts carrying vagrants' and the Edinburgh - Aberdeen express coach carrying Post Office mail. In 1811 some 1,500 carriages,

FORTH BRIDGE NORTH (Lac tum): 1952/3		
TRAIN	pass	DESTINATION
12.48 LEVEN	14.03	EDINBURGH (14.27)
12.27 Niddrie	14.06	Perth (16.15)
14.05 EDINBURGH	14.21	PERTH (15.34)
10.45 Aberdeen (Meat)	14.21	Kings Cross (01.35)
14.15 EDINBURGH	14.31	ABERDEEN (17.53)
13.35 Townhill Jcn	14.35	Niddrie (15.35)
13.05 Niddrie	14.44	Dundee via Cardenden (20.00)
13.50 STIRLING	15.00	EDINBURGH (15.19)
14.40 EDINBURGH	15.01	DUNDEE (17.34)
12.46 DUNDEE	15.13	EDINBURGH (15.35)
11.30 Camlachie	15.14	Burntisland (15.43)
14.45 THORNTON JCN	15.34	GLASGOW (16.45)
08.00 Carlisle	15.35	Perth (17.26)
12.30 Aberdeen (Fish)	15.43	Kings Cross (02.40)
14.00 Hardengreen	15.54	Thirnton Jcn (17.10)
12.40 ABERDEEN	15.57	EDINBURGH (16.20)
15.43 EDINBURGH	16.04	LADYBANK (17.25)
13.10 Perth (via Ladybank)	16.06	Niddrie (16.43)
14.30 CRAIL	16.21	GLASGOW (17.27)
16.05 EDINBURGH	16.26	PERTH (17.56)
14.49 DUNDEE	16.34	EDINBURGH (16.53)
16.15 EDINBURGH	16.34	ABERDEEN (20.23)
15.27 PERTH	16.41	EDINBURGH (17.00)
16.25 EDINBURGH	16.44	STIRLING (17.50)
13.40 Aberdeen (Fish)	16.58	Kings Cross (03.55)
16.07 GLASGOW	17.00	LEVEN (17.56)
16.25 BURNTISLAND	17.14	EDINBURGH (17.36)
16.03 STIRLING	17.20	EDINBURGH (17.43)
17.10 EDINBURGH	17.29	DUNDEE via CRAIL (20.15)
17.05 ROSYTH DOCKS	17.30	EDINBURGH (17.53)
16.13 GLASGOW	17.35	THORNTON JCN (18.26)
17.20 EDINBURGH	17.41	DUNDEE (19.45)
17.30 EDINBURGH	17.49	THORNTON JCN (18.48)
14.17 DUNDEE via CRAIL	17.51	EDINBURGH (18.13)
13.08 Dundee via Cardenden	18.10	Meadows (20.08)
17.13 GLASGOW	18.19	THORNTON JCN (19.04)
16.17 DUNDEE	18.26	EDINBURGH (18.48)
18.10 EDINBURGH	18.31	THORNTON JCN (19.25)
18.20 EDINBURGH	18.41	THORNTON JCN (19.33)
15.55 Dundee via Perth	18.51	Carlisle (23.41)
10.00 Heaton	18.51	Townhill Jcn (19.47)
18.50 EDINBURGH	19.06	ABERDEEN (22.32)
15.40 ABERDEEN	19.08	EDINBURGH (19.27)
18.55 EDINBURGH	19.11	PERTH (20.29)
17.36 PERTH	19.15	EDINBURGH (19.36)
18.05 Niddrie	19.19	Craiginches (23.12)
18.37 THORNTON JCN	19.25	GLASGOW (20.36)
18.20 Burntisland	19.39	Sighthill (23.20)
19.25 EDINBURGH	19.46	ANSTRUTHER (21.32)
19.38 Inverkeithing	19.52	Cadder (21.59)
18.35 Niddrie	19.56	Thornton Jcn (21.00)
11.35 Carlisle	20.14	Craiginches (01.45)
18.20 DUNDEE	20.34	EDINBURGH (20.56)
19.45 Leith Walk	20.45	Perth (22.35)
17.18 ABERDEEN	20.51	EDINBURGH (21.14)
19.37 GLASGOW	20.54	THORNTON JCN (21.43)
20.40 EDINBURGH	21.01	STIRLING (22.06)
19.58 THORNTON JCN	21.03	glasgow (22.17)
20.50 EDINBURGH	21.09	DUNDEE (23.01)
19.50 PERTH	21.10	EDINBURGH (21.29)
17.50 Aberdeen (Pcls)	23.14	Heaton (03.51)
21.20 EDINBURGH	21.41	LEVEN (22.49)
20.40 Leith Walk	21.53	Aberdeen (02.40)
20.45 LEVEN	21.53	EDINBURGH (22.12)

The Rosyth Dockyard line was opened in the early 1900s when this haven on the north shore of the Firth of Forth was being developed as a North Sea base for the Royal Navy, to counter the growing threat posed by the German High Seas Fleet. Rosyth Dockyard station, opened on 1st July 1915, had a long island platform capable of taking twelve coach trains, yet it was surprisingly narrow considering there were no restrictions on space. Three carriage sidings were provided on the north side. On 7th July 1957 B1 No.61146 arrived at Rosyth Dockyard with the 1.00pm Navy Day excursion from Cardenden. The most unusual backdrop consisted of Rosyth Castle, the Ferry Hills and the Forth Bridge. Wagons lurked amid naval paraphernalia in the foreground.

On 20th August 1959 J35 0-6-0 No.64496 toiled past Naval Base Junction with a workers train from Rosyth Dockyard to Edinburgh Waverley. B1 No.61101 took over at Inverkeithing. With their engine doing all the work, the crew had a spare moment to peer down at the photographer, although they seemed slightly bemused at becoming celebrities! Meanwhile an unidentified V2 pounded across Jamestown viaduct on the climb to the Forth Bridge with the 3.29pm from Perth to Edinburgh Waverley. Having emerged from Ferry Toll tunnel, the Rosyth line joined the North Queensferry branch at this point and the track became double to Inverkeithing.

done and the powers lapsed. They tried again in 1853 but again there was no progress. By 1863 both the Edinburgh & Glasgow and North British companies regarded the passage as a vital link and presented Bills to purchase it as well as build connecting lines. Parliament recognised the urgency of having the ferry in railway ownership and decided in favour of the North British. However, the dithering continued and after two years powers were relinquished to the Edinburgh

The first bridge proposed by Thomas Bouch would have reached the north bank of the Firth of Forth at Charlestown, no doubt giving this relatively obscure coastal settlement some prominence. Charlestown harbour was built around 1800 and exported coal brought down by the Earl of Elgin's horse-operated waggonway. After a complex history of reconstruction and realignment, a conventional branch line was created and Dunfermline - Charlestown passenger services ran from 1894 to 1926. On 26th December 1961 the small brick built terminus on the sea wall (out of sight along the shore and devoid of track) survived as a dwelling as snowplough-fitted J35 0-6-0 No.64525 prepared to leave with the daily trip freight to Dunfermline Townhill Yard. Charlestown presented a bleak scene on this occasion, exacerbated by bitter weather and a sprinkling of snow. Former limekilns on the left were derelict, as was most of the harbour, and several steam trawlers were being broken up in the Metal Industries Ltd scrapyard on the right. The J35 had picked up seven gunpowder vans from Crombie Naval Stores Depot and these constituted the whole train on this grey Boxing Day.

& Glasgow. The matter was finally settled when the companies amalgamated during 1865 and the boats became North British property on 19th September 1867. Meanwhile there had been progress with the southern connecting line, opened from Ratho to Dalmeny on 1st March 1866 and reaching South Queensferry on 1st June 1868. The junction with the main line was just east of the existing Ratho station so a new low level platform (quarter of a mile from the junction) was required. From here the single track swung northwards past Newbridge, gently dropping from about 150ft to just over 100ft where it spanned the River Almond. Immediately afterwards a station served the village of Kirkliston (a mile and three quarters). This was followed by a steady climb up to 200ft at Craigbrae, accomplished by means of cuttings and a long embankment. Dalmeny station (four miles) was followed by substantial excavations and a severe curve as the branch dropped down to the shoreline at South Queensferry (five and a half miles). The terminus lasted just over ten years, for it was replaced by a new through station when a short extension to the recently improved Port Edgar harbour (six miles) opened on 1st October 1878. North Queensferry acquired a seven mile branch from Dunfermline on 1st November 1877. By Inverkeithing this was already less than 50ft above sea level but after skirting Inverkeithing Inner Bay, it was faced with Ferry Hills and a tunnel was required through tough volcanic rock. The line terminated on the pier. Completion of the Forth Bridge in 1890 virtually destroyed traffic on the ancient ferry crossing and operations were handed over to a Bo'ness contractor (assisted by a subsidy) during 1893. In 1898 an observer reported little activity 'save a cyclist now and then, and a few tramps in various conditions of life'. However, a steady increase in road traffic gave the ferry an importance which, it was thought, the bridge had dispelled for ever. The North British resumed working it on 13th November 1919 and purchased DUNDEE, a 264 ton ferry capable of taking nearly a thousand passengers and, more significantly, ten cars or three lorries with two cars. Inevitably, both connecting branches were affected by the Forth Bridge. Passenger services from Dalmeny to Port Edgar and Inverkeithing to North Queensferry were withdrawn on 5th March 1890, although new stations at Dalmeny and North Queensferry were opened on the bridge approach lines. Port Edgar was an important base for escort craft and minesweepers in World War I with a consequent increase in traffic on the South Queensferry branch - this also applied during World War II. South Queensferry station on the Port Edgar extension reopened for passengers as South Queensferry Halt on 1st December 1919

The Firth of Forth narrows to less than a mile and a half at Queensferry and was obviously the best place for a bridge. However, the water is up to 200ft deep and construction would probably have been impossible without the volcanic outcrop forming Inchgarvie island. The seabed here is like an inverted two arch viaduct, mirroring the lower part of the bridge. Inchgarvie cantilever, in the centre of this view, clearly shows the main elements of the design, notably the cluster of four piers, the screwjack and the main tower - nevertheless it would take a structural engineer to fully comprehend the logic behind the bewildering array of diagonal tubes and lattice girders forming the limbs of the cantilevers. The two link spans look as if they had been lifted into place, but each weighs 872 tons and were, in fact, built as extensions of the cantilevers. Car ferry QUEEN MARGARET, heading for North Queensferry, passed close to the magnificent Forth Bridge on 21st August 1964, with the solitary pier of Bouch's abortive suspension viaduct visible to the left of the Inchgarvie cantilever. At least it has found employment, as the base for a lighthouse!

and a modest service was maintained until 14th January 1929. Ratho Low Level - Dalmeny passenger trains ceased on 22nd September 1930. A goods service ran to North Queensferry pier until 4th October 1954, and most of the branch was still intact in 1994 as it provided access to Rosyth Dockyard. Dalmeny goods closed on 24th February 1964 and the pick up serving Kirkliston yard, the nearby distillery sidings and South Queensferry ceased on 7th February 1966.

Inverkeithing yard was the last to go, on 11th September 1967. By this time a momentous development had revolutionised the Queensferry passage. On 4th September 1964 Her Majesty the Queen opened the Forth Road Bridge and after 900 years the ferries finally finished. Queensferry is still a special place, with a constant roar from the road bridge, a frequent rumble from the railway girders, and ghosts of the ferries haunting the slipways.

THE FORTH BRIDGE

A bridge over the Firth of Forth was suggested during the early 1700s, but this was clearly ahead of its time. In 1805 an Edinburgh engineer proposed a double tunnel 'one for comers and one for goers' and invited the public to subscribe to its estimated £164,000 cost - alas, to no avail. During 1818 a bridge primarily for stagecoaches was mooted. It was to have three main spans of 1,500ft, suspended from 190ft towers and approached over rocky piers blending with the adjacent volcanic outcrops. The design inspired little confidence and was soon dismissed. To quote an Edwardian writer 'the bridge would no doubt have presented a very light and slender appearance, so light in fact that on a dull day it would hardly have been visible, and after a severe gale might no longer be seen, even on a clear day'. With railway interest growing, Thomas Bouch came on the scene and soon suggested an astonishing three mile bridge from Blackness Castle to Charlestown, with 62 lattice girder spans, four of which would be 500ft long. He enthused about the relative cheapness of the scheme but had not anticipated the treacherous shifting sands of the seabed, which rendered construction impossible. Almost immediately a sequence of events made a bridge essential rather then desirable. Firstly, the Edinburgh, Perth & Dundee and Edinburgh & Glasgow merged with the North British, creating a unified network split by the Firth of Forth. Operating the Granton ferry was costing £30,000 a year plus £4,000 in pier duties to the Duke of Buccleuch, goods were being damaged during transhipment, and of the 550 wagons handled on an average day no less than a hundred were suffering delay. Secondly, the Scottish Central and Scottish North Eastern lines, which had hitherto provided a neutral route to the north open to other companies, amalgamated with the Caledonian to the virtual exclusion of outsiders. The North British was forced to rely on its Granton ferries which could not cope, and many passengers deserted them.

Bouch came to the rescue, with plans for a huge suspension bridge at Queensferry, and the Forth Bridge Railway Company duly received its Act on 5th August 1873. Mighty steel towers 550ft high were to support twin 1,600ft spans giving a 150ft headway for shipping.

Cantilever construction was not invented for the Forth Bridge and, indeed, a primitive timber version was put up over a river in Tibet over 300 years ago. It was the sheer scale of construction which made the Scottish structure such an engineering landmark and the design was subsequently copied for railway bridges elsewhere in the world. Even the approach viaducts and tall piers receiving the outer ends of two of the cantilevers were mighty undertakings. At Hawes Pier, South Queensferry, on 15th August 1961 the ferry QUEEN MARGARET was about to leave for the north shore. She shared the work with sister vessels MARY QUEEN OF SCOTS, ROBERT THE BRUCE and SIR WILLIAM WALLACE. Former Denny shipyard tug/tender THE SECOND SNARK was departing on a cruise. This vessel, now owned by Clyde Marine Motoring Co. Ltd. and based at Greenock Princes Pier, still cruised on the Clyde in 1994.

Standard 2-6-4T No.80007 emerging from the south cantilever of the Forth Bridge with the 1.40pm Sunday local from Kirkcaldy to Edinburgh Waverley, on 18th August 1963.

hanging sections are balanced and strong enough to carry their own weight and any load put on them without extra supports. Three cantilevers were employed, the centre one standing on Inchgarvie island. Each of them rises from clusters of four piers set in the estuary bed and most of the weight of the bridge is dispersed through these largely submerged columns. They are 70ft in diameter at the base, 50ft at the top and vary from 20ft to 90ft in height. The four South Queensferry piers had to go deep into boulder clay to achieve stability and presented considerable difficulties. Massive caissons were built on the shore, then floated out and sunk; these had special chambers at the base, reached through an air lock, and Italians with the necessary expertise worked in compressed air to excavate material to the required depth. The interior cavity was then filled with 17,000 tons of concrete and the giant monoliths were faced with Aberdeen granite.

Fixing the four immense steel tubes forming the centre of each cantilever to the stone piers was one of the biggest difficulties. This was achieved by constructing large iron boxes called screwjacks, each of which was secured by 48 bolts embedded 24ft into the stonework. The 12ft diameter main tubes, diagonal bracing tubes and curved base tubes then rose from the screwjacks. No less than 54,000 tons of best steel was used in the structure and every other statistic concerning the bridge is equally impressive. Forty miles of plates with a surface area of 135 acres made up the tubes; 6,500,000 rivets held the metal together; 740,000 cubic feet of granite was used in the piers

There were actually to be two parallel bridges, one for each track, with the lattice girder decks braced together by diagonal struts. The central towers would have risen up from Inchgarvie island in the middle of the Firth. Raising sufficient capital was a problem at first, although guarantees were made by the North Eastern, Great Northern and Midland companies, reflecting the battle for Anglo-Scottish traffic throughout the length of Britain. Contracts were let in 1877, a construction site was established and work began in 1878. One of the brick piers on Inchgarvie was completed, enabling Bouch and his backers to sail out and lay the ceremonial foundation stone, but the collapse of the Tay Bridge at the end of 1879 immediately halted any further progress. Moreover, the Board of Trade questioned the use of the suspension principle for such a large railway structure. A bridge across the Firth seemed as far away as ever. In 1881 attempts were made to abandon the whole scheme, but the English partners raised strong objections and there was a firm commitment to pursue the project.

After consultations with the most eminent engineers in the land, a second Forth Bridge Railway Act was passed in July 1882. Contracts were signed on 21st December 1882 and work resumed during April 1883. The cantilever principle

was to be employed, and although this term is frequently used in connection with the bridge, it may need some explanation: the main girder structures are supported in the centre by huge towers and the over-

This unusual view from the end of the South Queensferry cantilever gives an impression of the dizzy heights which construction workers had to get used to. Over 50 of them sacrificed their lives while the bridge was being built. Two of the Forth ferries and THE SECOND SNARK can be seen at South Queensferry pier, whilst Dalmeny station - actually called Forth Bridge for a few weeks - can be seen in the distance. The date was 18th August 1963.

About to cross the Forth Bridge on 1st August 1953, Black Five 4-6-0 No.45180 heads the 3.10pm train from Perth to Edinburgh Waverley. Photograph Brian Morrison.

off westwards from the North Queensferry branch through a re-sited Inverkeithing station and climbed through a 386 yard tunnel beneath the town. It then occupied a shelf high above Inverkeithing Inner Bay before curving south eastwards across Jamestown viaduct, which consisted of four deep lattice girder spans and a stone arch. The 1 in 70 ascent continued through the 569 yard North Queensferry tunnel, hacked out of the tough volcanic rock of the Ferry Hills, and these two miles of difficult roadbed met the bridge just south of the new North Queensferry station. On the south side, lines were built from Dalmeny on the South Queensferry branch to Winchburgh Junction and Saughton Junction on the Edinburgh - Glasgow main line. The former, four and a half miles in length, described a confident sweeping curve north of Kirkliston with plenty of earthworks and bridges but neither tunnels nor viaducts. The latter, five and a quarter miles long, was equally bold and pursued a gently curving course across the River Almond meadows and the lingering slopes of Corstorphine Hill. Its intermediate station at Turnhouse closed on 22nd September 1930, but this loss has since been offset by the opening of South Gyle on 9th May 1985, to serve new housing and subsequently a large 'out of town' shopping complex. The immediate approach to the Forth Bridge on the south side was relatively straightforward, comprising just three quarters of a mile of cutting and embankment together with a new Dalmeny station.

Construction work on the Forth Bridge was concluded on 6th November 1889, although testing and inspection had to follow before it opened for traffic. Per-

and approach viaducts. The ends of the north and south cantilevers are 1 mile 23 yards apart and the total length, including approach viaducts, is 1 mile 1,005 yards. There are two spans of 1,710ft over the main channels and two of 675ft towards the respective shorelines. There is a headway of 157ft above high water mark, and the extreme height from the base of the deepest pier to the top of the cantilever is 451ft. The bridge cost £2,500,000 and 5000 men were employed at the peak of construction. Maximum publicity was achieved during the work, with the structure featuring widely on postcards, pottery and other souvenirs.

Although almost wholly overshadowed by the bridge itself, the approach lines were substantial undertakings in their own right. On the north side, a new line was built along the coast between Inverkeithing and Burntisland, whilst another threaded its way between Mawcarse and Bridge of Earn through precipitous Glenfarg, providing direct routes to Dundee and Perth respectively. The actual Forth Bridge Railway veered

Ex-LNER K4 2-6-0 No.61998 MACLEOD OF MACLEOD came off the Forth Bridge and eased into Dalmeny on 11th June 1960 with the 7.10pm relief from Ladybank to Edinburgh Waverley. The train was specially provided for daytrippers, including Sunday School parties, returning from popular resorts such as Kinghorn, Burntisland and Aberdour on this fine summer Saturday evening. Six of these Gresley moguls were built for the West Highland line in 1937/38 but fell out of favour and finished their days at Thornton shed.

haps the most demanding test was the positioning of two trains, each consisting of three locomotives and fully laden wagons of pig iron, side by side on the outer ends of the cantilevers. This 1,804 ton burden caused no problems whatsoever, and minor deflections of the girders were precisely as expected. Afterwards the Board of Trade inspector came along and praised the 'thoroughly good workmanship'. The Forth Bridge was opened with great ceremony during a howling gale on 4th March 1890 but the only passenger trains to use it over the next three months were Edinburgh - Dunfermline locals, for the approach lines were incomplete. On 2nd June 1890 the routes from Burntisland, Winchburgh and Saughton finally began to carry trains and a phenomenal success story had begun.

Traffic across the bridge soon reached epic proportions and caused horrendous problems until the line from Saughton Junction through Waverley was quadrupled, as noted earlier. The North British, North Eastern, Great Northern and Midland companies had invested wisely and the East Coast route to northern Scotland gained a tremendous advantage over its West Coast competitors. Despite the haemorrhage of traffic from rail to road this mighty feat of engineering still carries plenty of trains. In 1990 its centenary was celebrated and the steelwork is now illuminated by floodlights on summer evenings. The structure is also in perfect condition - surely one of the best tributes possible to the Victorian railway builders.

The northern approach to the Forth Bridge was remarkably similar to that from Dalmeny, although a tall signal box at the beginning of the viaduct provided added interest. Electric lights on decorative posts illuminated North Queensferry station, rather than the old oil lamps converted to gas remaining at Dalmeny around the same time, and the staff seemed particularly interested in horticulture. As an east coast haar (sea fog) began to close in, work-soiled Gresley A3 Pacific No.60035 WINDSOR LAD rolled down the gradient through North Queensferry with the 5.25pm Edinburgh Waverley to Dundee Tay Bridge, on 20th August 1959. Note the scissors crossing, enabling wrong line working during track maintenance. Another one was provided at the south end.

The rugged civil engineering of the Forth Bridge and its approaches was hardly reflected by the three stations on the new line. Nevertheless they were pleasant timber structures, featuring lots of detailed panelling, framework bargeboards with finials, and attractive canopies in the current North British style. On 20th August 1959 B1 4-6-0 No.61148 made a smoky exit from North Queensferry tunnel with the 2.15pm from Dundee Tay Bridge to Edinburgh Waverley via Crail, watched by a trio of scouts. In 1994 the up side building at North Queensferry was still more or less in original condition, although the down side structure (on the left) had been replaced by a signal relay room, embellished with murals of the bridge.

With the Forth Bridge in the background, very smart Jubilee 4-6-0 No.45724 WARSPITE of Carlisle Kingmoor shed approached Dalmeny North Junction with the 3.36pm from Thornton Junction to Glasgow Queen Street. This was a most unusual working for such an engine, although it was Glasgow Fair Monday when all manner of odd arrangements were necessary. The South Queensferry branch is in the cutting on the right.

Peppercorn A2 Pacific No.60525 A.H. PEPPERCORN powered confidently past Dalmeny North Junction with the twelve coach 4.17pm from Edinburgh Waverley to Aberdeen on 20th July 1959. The South Queensferry branch passes behind the signal box whilst the line to Winchburgh Junction, used by Glasgow trains, is on the right.

The massive scale of the Forth Bridge approach lines was particularly apparent at Jamestown viaduct, between Inverkeithing and North Queensferry. B1 4-6-0 No.61343 slogged up the 1 in 70 climb towards the bridge with the 2.48pm Dundee Tay Bridge to Edinburgh Waverley on 20th August 1959. A plume of smoke just visible above the cab roof is not some previously unrecorded form of booster but, more prosaically, the emission from a factory chimney. Present day photographers are unlikely to be troubled by such signs of industry! Out of sight, in a cutting deep below the nearest girder span, are the Rosyth Dockyard branch and trackbed of the first line to North Queensferry.

D11 4-4-0 No.62677 EDIE OCHILTREE took the Dunfermline line at Inverkeithing on 2nd August 1958 with the 6.32pm Glasgow Buchanan Street to Thornton Junction. These trains normally started at Queen Street, but were being temporarily diverted because of signalling and track alterations. Again, the haar sea mist was closing in around the north shore of the Firth of Forth.

Sir Nigel Gresley's last design was a lightweight mixed traffic 2-6-2 which would have replaced numerous pre-grouping 4-4-0, 4-4-2 and 4-6-0 classes. Two of these V4s entered service in 1941. The first V4 (BR No.61700) carried the name BANTAM COCK but the second was officially anonymous. However, No.61701 was always nicknamed BANTAM HEN and the Aberdeen Ferryhill loco is seen here heading through Inverkeithing with a southbound livestock train, on 10th August 1957. Such traffic has long since been lost to road transport.

Seen from the overbridge just south of Inverkeithing station on 2nd August 1958, the 6.45pm from Edinburgh Waverley to Dundee Tay Bridge passed Inverkeithing South Junction signal box, appropriately with A1 Pacific No.60159 BONNIE DUNDEE in charge. The North Queensferry branch dropped away gently to the left, but somewhat enigmatically the Forth Bridge Railway had to tunnel beneath the town in order to gain height. This scene has changed considerably, for the signal box and goods yards have been swept away, the single track Rosyth Dockyard branch now leaves the main line on this side of the bridge, and new housing developments are evident.

Inverkeithing Central Junction, about a quarter of a mile north of Inverkeithing station, was where the new line to Burntisland diverged from the original North Queensferry branch. On 10th August 1957 D30 4-4-0 No.62436 LORD GLENVARLOCH came off the latter with the 5.56pm from Dunfermline Lower to Inverkeithing, providing connections for Edinburgh, Glasgow and Thornton Junction. A triangle was formed by the avoiding line between Inverkeithing North Junction and Inverkeithing East Junction. Woodland in the background marked the secluded grounds of historic Pitreavie House, although the peace and quiet is now disturbed by the M90 motorway.

It was hot and hazy on 20th August 1959 and virtually every carriage window was open as Peppercorn A2 Pacific No.60532 BLUE PETER passed Inverkeithing Central Junction with the 12.40pm express from Aberdeen to Edinburgh Waverley. The original alignment of the North Queensferry branch is represented by the line on the extreme left.

On 16th November 1956 Edinburgh said goodbye to its trams and decorated car No.172 passed the George IV statue at the junction of Hanover Street and George Street, during the final hours of operation. Since then the capital has had to rely heavily on road transport, especially after most of the remaining suburban stations and lines closed. Lothian Region Transport provides a very good bus service but the city suffers from acute traffic problems at times. Although there has been much talk about rapid transit schemes, dedicated busways and even a revived suburban railway network, so far very little has been done. Glasgow is a showpiece for local train services and Newcastle has its splendid Metro, whilst Manchester and Sheffield have brought back the trams with considerable success. Meanwhile Edinburgh has a comprehensive network of footpaths along old trackbeds. Maybe one day...?